To Mary,
Make today
a happy memory
for tomorrow.
Betty

And how was your day?

Betty Jean Robb

Dageforde Publishing, Inc.

ISBN: 1-886225-31-1
Library of Congress Number: 98-71483

Cover Art by C.M. Zuby

Dageforde Publishing, Inc.
941 'O' Street, Suite 706
Lincoln, Nebraska 68508-1809
(402) 475-1123
http://www.dageforde.com
email: info@dageforde.com

Printed in the United States of America
10 9 8 7 6 5 4 3 2 1

*T*his book has no plot. It is a book filled with warm and humorous anecdotes. It is dotted, here and there, with wanderings and thoughts into the past and the future.

It is about a woman who, day by day, sees the joy and humor in growing older. It is about life in a small community. It is about the love of family and friends.

All things considered, happiness and contentment are ours if we look forward to each day, for each day will bring something new or remembered within and around us.

June

June 10. I can remember when sixty-five was just a speed limit. Now, it has become my age. I know this is a strange date to start a journal, but I'm old enough to do whatever I want.

June 11. School is out for the summer. Our seven-year-old grandson Sam went home today after a two-week visit. I've learned the names of the Ninja turtles, that really good water guns are expensive, and that when buying a rubber snake, you have to line them up on the floor in the store to see which one looks most lifelike.

June 12. Eight years ago, my husband Bob and I moved to town after living on a farm that was sixteen miles from town for thirty-six years. I'm still adjusting to one thing. As hard as I try, even in summer, I can't go to the grocery store without stocking up for a month ahead—just in case we have a blizzard. Today,

I have twenty-four rolls of toilet tissue, eighteen bars of soap, five boxes of tissue, ten boxes of cereal, eight cans of ripe olives, eight pounds of coffee, nine pounds of butter, four bottles of laundry detergent, three bottles of bleach, four bottles of dish detergent, four cans each of spinach, asparagus, beans, corn and beets, five cans each of apricots, peaches, plums, pineapple and pears, and all kinds of mixes too numerous to count. I quit cooking from scratch the day the first cake mix was introduced on the market. My point is that we only need enough for two people in the house now, only half as much as we did when we lived on the farm, and that we now live only six blocks from the grocery store, so why do I do this?

Six blocks will get you almost any place you want to go in our small western Nebraska town of Big Springs. From north to south, there are five blocks and from east to west, there are twelve blocks. At the last census, the count was up to 495 of mostly good people living here. Our little town is a well-kept secret. Most of the world, including greater Nebraska, doesn't know we're here.

I like my life in this small, easy-going town. We have a grocery store, gas station, bank, library, post office, grain elevator, garage repair shop, a connected elementary and high school, a combination hardware store and lumber yard, three churches, a cemetery, a small four-day-a-week medical clinic, tavern, fire hall, police station, barber shop, beauty salon, two parks, a softball diamond, a swimming pool, a museum and a bed and breakfast hotel. I can't fathom living in a city and always wonder why all those people are in such a hurry and where they're going at that fast pace. I have a strong suspicion they're looking for the street that takes them out of the city and on the road to Big Springs.

June 13. I went to a neighborhood birthday coffee this morning. Should any of us want to know a person's age, I have a friend Pat who has a unique way of finding out. She strolls through the cemetery and if that person has planned well ahead, there is their birth date, etched in stone.

June 14. Every summer, I'm fascinated by our neighbors Ed and Loree, who live kitty-corner across the block from us. They love gardening. At the first sign of spring, they're busy preparing their huge backyard for the vegetables and fruits of summer. I watch from our kitchen window as they plant, pull weeds, hoe, water, harvest and share the bounty of their labors with others. This in itself is not amazing, except that they're eighty-seven and seventy-nine years of age. Loree, being the younger, does her gardening for hours on end, bent over from the waist down. Were that me, I'd walk around permanently in an inverted V, which might be a good position to be in, if your career was worm digging.

June 15. When Bob comes home, he greets our three pets first before he says hello to me. We have a basset hound named Sophie and a toy poodle named Killer who's Bob's personal bodyguard. I wanted to name him Julio, which I think may have given him a gentler outlook on the world. Our third pet is a white dove named Cuckoo who truly laughs and considers me the other woman in Bob's life. I think I understand why they're greeted before I am. It's because I don't wiggle all over with joy, whine in anticipation of a pat, nor coo in lovesick awe, the minute Bob appears at the door.

June 16. Nothing will make you feel older than mentioning Betty Grable, Harry James, Alan Ladd or

3

Veronica Lake in a casual conversation and receiving a blank stare in return.

June 17. I miss having our son Kevin live close enough to us to fix things around the house when they're in need of repair. He didn't inherit this quality from his father. I recall the time our toilet wouldn't flush properly. Bob's solution was to jiggle the handle, turn on the cold water tap in the sink, then flush. Miraculously, it actually worked, but eventually we tired of the ritual and called the plumber.

June 18. It's Fathers' Day and Bob is fixing the lawn sprinklers. He mowed over two of them earlier this year and replaced them himself to save money. One of them shoots a fine spray of water, straight out of our yard and into the alley. I'm not brave enough to look to see where the other sprinkler is sprinkling.

June 19. Bob doesn't think much of my filing system. Recently, he was replacing the cutting line on our yard trimmer and was looking for instructions in the file. He asked if they were filed under T for trimmer or W for weed-eater or E for edger. I said, "Of course not. They're filed under I for instructions."

June 20. As I looked in the mirror this morning, I noticed I seem to be getting more wrinkles every day. It's true, I've earned them but I feel like I don't deserve them. They seem like cruel and unusual punishment for something I don't remember doing.

June 21. My friend Vy has a birthday on this beautiful first day of summer. Ah, summer. Warm days, picnics, fishing, flowers in bloom, going outside without a coat, fresh garden vegetables, moonlight strolls, Sunday drives, birds singing. Oh, summer. Mosquitoes, flies, bugs, weeds, mowing, discovering last year's summer clothes have shrunk, nights too hot to sleep. I hate summer.

June 22. My daughter Robin and I have lots in common. For instance, we don't celebrate the birthday of the person who invented the cooking stove. I did send her the following recipe.

Boiling water
Turn stove on high heat. Measure in measuring cup,
2 cups of water. Put water in a 1 quart saucepan and place on hot burner. When the water bubbles, it is done. Use potholder to remove from heat. Leftovers may be stored in the refrigerator. At this time, there is no instant hot water mix on the market, although it may be available in the future.

June 23. Today is my friend June's birthday. She holds a nice trim weight. I finally lost that one pound I've been trying to lose for several weeks. Now I only need to lose ten more and I'll be at the weight I'm aiming for. I guess I'll reward myself with a banana split.

June 24. I painted the bedroom walls today. The color doesn't seem quite right. I know what my friend Margaret would say. She'd remind me of the time, years ago, when we lived on the farm and I wasn't satisfied with the shade of the paint I was using. Rather than drive 16 miles to town to have color added, I poured a whole bottle of maple flavoring into the paint. It didn't do much for the color, but the walls really smelled good for a few days.

June 25. Don't you hate it when you run into someone who knows you and you can't remember ever having even seen the person before? Do you try and fake through it like I do, with the hope that someone will come along and call them by name, so you will at least have a clue? The alternative is to spend the next few days trying to remember who he or she was until eventually you forget what it was you were trying to remember in the first place.

June 26. This morning I stopped to chat with Doris, who is a friend who also happens to be a relative. Good friends and good relatives are like a pair of shoes. They become more comfortable the longer you have them. Our friends and relatives wear well and unlike shoes, they won't be discarded when they're worn out and run down at the heels.

Speaking of relatives, everyone has at least one they'd rather not claim. I have a standard comment for this problem. Whether they're Bob's relatives or mine, I always say they're his. I figure he inherited mine by marriage.

June 27. Regardless of age, a great number of females in Big Springs wisely don shorts when the weather turns hot. I've foregone this pleasure as I'm well aware my knees resemble two pumpkins perched atop two fence posts. Today I got brave and put on a pair of shorts, but was hesitant to leave the safety of our home. Eventually, the time came when I needed to take a bag of smelly garbage to the dumpster.

As I felt sure all the neighbors had been waiting for this grand exit, I hit upon the solution for saving all of us embarrassment. There was one, tiny cloud in the sky, so I simply wore my long raincoat over my shorts to escape any undue notice on my journey to the dumpster.

June 28. I never help Bob with mowing the lawn, but today, I even surprised myself. I helped mow and even wore my shorts while doing it. Kathy, our friend, neighbor, and relative, drove by, stopped her car, backed up, and yelled out the window, "Betty, is this a snapshot moment?"

I yelled back, "No, it's just one of my weaker moments."

June 29. I'm a crossword puzzle addict. I do my puzzles with a pen so people will think I'm smart. No one has ever been interested enough to look closely to see if the words I put down make any sense. Until they do, xmau works fine as a four-letter word for a Turkish regiment.

June 30. The wall plaque in our living room greets guests with the words "Welcome. One beautiful person and one old grouch live here." When guests want to know which one of us is the beautiful person and which one is the grouch, I tell them that it depends on the day. Today is my turn to be the grouch. Why? Just because I want to be, that's why.

July 1. Today is my sister-in-law Jean's birthday. She is my jigsaw puzzle buddy. When she and I get started on a jigsaw puzzle, all else in the outside world ceases to exist until we have it completed. Jigsaw puzzles are like potato chips and peanuts. You can't stop with just one piece.

July 2. To most people, this wouldn't be a memorable day. Bob has a trait that's remarkable. He has an unbelievable memory for dates. Like today, he informed me that fifty years ago on July 2nd he had an appendectomy. With a memory like that, why is it that later today he forgot to bring the mail home and made three trips to pick it up before he actually got it into the house?

July 3. "Act your age" my mother always told me, but sometimes I forgot. On my 62nd birthday, I was racing the neighborhood kindergarten children in the street a block from our home. I almost won, but in my final burst of speed, I fell and broke my arm. My first concern wasn't my arm, though. It was to quickly look around to see how many of my neighbors had seen me in this very unladylike position.

July 4. The Fourth of July is a much quieter and safer holiday than it once was. When Robin and Kevin were small, we always invited our relatives to the farm for the day. We had a picnic, played games, and in the evening, we had our own display of fireworks. Bob, his dad, and my dad were in charge of lighting the firecrackers, Roman candles, sky bursts, sparklers and twirling pinwheels.

One year, my dad even added an impromptu dance to the entertainment which we all applauded. Later, we learned he wasn't trying to amuse us. A twirling pinwheel had shot up his trouser leg and he was only trying to put it out.

July 5. Doris took Pat, Marge, Elaine, LaRae, and me with her to visit the iris farm north of Julesburg, Colorado. There were six hundred varieties of iris and they were all beautiful. We all ordered bulbs for our own yards.

Margaret E. was taking our orders and someone asked her where we should pick up our bulbs. She said, "You can pick them up at my home in Julesburg. Betty knows where I live."

I should know because I grew up in Julesburg, so I said, "Of course, that will be fine." I wonder how the other ladies will react later when I tell them that I have absolutely no idea where she lives. I was just too embarrassed to say so.

July 6. At least one hundred trains pass by Big Springs daily. We live close to the railroad tracks. Everyone who lives in Big Springs lives close to the railroad tracks. I'm looking for 149 volunteers who will help me, under cover of darkness, reroute the tracks to a location ten miles in any direction from where they are now. Maybe, someone could invent a silent train whistle that cars react to in the same way dogs react to silent dog whistles. Maybe, the tracks could be replaced with conveyer belts. Maybe, the trains could run in underground tunnels. Maybe, some night, the neighbors will see me running through the streets in my nightgown toward the railroad tracks, screaming, "I can't take it anymore," brandishing a sledgehammer in an upraised arm.

July 7. My daughter Robin's birthday is today. She's my favorite short person and I miss her. We do our best, though, to keep the telephone company from filing for bankruptcy.

Robin teaches school in Red Cloud, Nebraska, goes to summer college, sings beautifully for public functions, tutors people, and, as a single parent, is raising my fantastic teenage grandchildren, Michael and Jillian. Now, if she could just find something to do with that extra half-hour that must be left over at the end of the day.

July 8. Bob has a language all his own that Robin, Kevin and I have deciphered after many years of repetition. Here are a few phrases we have translated and the appropriate times they are used.

1. "Like I say, when a big flock of bird dogs comes a-flying over" is to be said when there's a long pause in a conversation.

2. "That's the way the old ball bounces" is to be used whenever things aren't going right.

3. "Colder than a well-digger's bottom" pertains to really cold weather.

4. "Fall in, in a column of deuces" means it's time to leave.

5. "Whoop!Whoop! Whoop!" We're still working on this one because it means anything from "You're siting in my chair" to "Watch out. There's a semi-truck headed straight for us!"

July 9. Computerized equipment drives me crazy. The electricity went off for a few minutes a week ago and the digital clock on our VCR just blinks at me. Once before, I tried to set it following the instruction booklet. I ended up with the correct time flashing intermittently on the television screen while the VCR clock blinked blankly.

Can staring at something like that hypnotize you? I hope not, because it won't get set properly until Michael comes to visit and fix it for us. By then, I should know if hypnosis can be self-induced or not.

July 10. If dreams have a hidden meaning, I'm worried about the one Bob had last night. He dreamed he heard me scream and there was a strange woman standing by the bed holding a fly swatter and motioning him to be quiet. In his dream, he arose to see a stranger and me dueling with fly swatters in the kitchen. He actually did awaken then to find himself in the hall headed for the kitchen.

My first thought when he told me about it over breakfast in the morning was that the dream meant he was my protector. My next thought was, "Which one of us did he really intend to defend?"

July 11. Walking is good exercise. I believe that, but I haven't been very successful at it. I tried group walking and soon discovered that the majority of the group had longer legs than I do. Therefore, I had to take two steps to their one, so I really felt I only needed to walk half as far as they did to achieve the same results. Strolling is actually my preference.

July 12. My miracle worker Tiny gave me a permanent today. Does anyone remember that the process when getting a permanent forty years ago was a day in a torture chamber? You were hung by the hair with electric wires attached to a head-shaped oven designed to prevent you from scratching that itch that would invariably appear on your big toe. I was sure I'd come out looking like Medusa and sometimes I did.

July 13. A voice spoke to me from above. It said, "I created restaurants for people like you." I said, "I already know that. Don't tell me. Tell Bob."

July 14. The last time I complained about my hair turning gray, my granddaughter, Jillian, tried to cheer me up. She said, "Grandma, you have a right to have gray hair. Think of all that you have lived through. You've lived through three wars, and wasn't Franklin Roosevelt a president in your lifetime and wasn't—"

I interrupted her, "Stop Jillian. You've cheered me up enough."

July 15. Our son, Kevin, is one of those rare people with an infectious laugh, and I miss hearing his laughter. My hearing is good, but not that good. He, his wife Mary, and their three children live six hours away.

Kevin also has a gift for telling anecdotes that make the stories bigger and better than life. When he was ten years old, he came riding his bike home at a high rate of speed, jumped off, and ran into the house yelling, "Mom, there's a giant jack rabbit in the neighbor's field." I replied, "That's nice," and continued with my housework. Many years later, my friend Margaret told me that she'd seen it, too. To this day, I wonder what I would've seen had I bothered to go see for myself.

July 16. Jillian is fourteen years old today. That is to say, she's fourteen going on eighteen. She's pretty, charming, and witty. I hope her sense of humor is with her when she finds out I've painted over her growing marks on our kitchen wall.

Robin, Jillian, and I saw a pair of silver slippers at a garage sale a while ago that were circa 1930. She thought they were "totally hideous." I brought them home and mailed them to her for her birthday. Happy birthday, Jillian.

July 17. Have you ever noticed that as we age our necks are compared to fowl? Swan necks are for the young. As we grow older, we have the chicken neck, the turkey neck, and the dreaded pelican neck. I'm at the turk-hen neck stage now.

July 18. The only thing I miss about living on the farm is the peace and quiet. If more than one vehicle drove by a day, it was cause for celebration.

The neighbors were great. Melvin and Margaret, Gene and Alice, Henry and Lorrie, Herman and Esther, and Bob and Audrey were our closest neighbors. We all lived at least a mile and a half from each other.

Farm neighbors are always there with a helping hand. One stormy night, I was home alone. Lorrie called to warn me there was a suspicious man on foot headed toward our farm. Being petrified of guns, I grabbed a flashlight and a hammer. The man walked on by but when Bob came home, I told him about it. He questioned my choice of weapons and just shook his head when I explained, "I was going to shine the flashlight in his face, then hit him on the head with the hammer."

July 19. Farm wives are required to help their husbands with farm chores at times. Bob didn't ask for my help unless it was a necessity after I tried to drive the truck and all I could accomplish was driving in circles in reverse in the farm yard. He stopped me and politely told me he'd do the farm work if I'd limit myself to less complicated chores.

Another time, I was asked to drive the pickup that was loaded with wire and drive ahead of Bob in the field while he put up fence. I put the kids in the pickup, got behind the wheel, and away we went. When we got to the field, Bob waved and I waved back. I was feeling really proud of myself until Robin and Kevin told me, "Daddy is still waving with his hands." I don't know what all the fuss was about; I was only a mile off course. They really should print universal standard hand-signal manuals for farm wives.

July 20. My fantasy is to be a contestant on "Wheel of Fortune." I can call for a consonant or buy a vowel with the best of them—when I'm at home. If I could talk them into letting me take our sofa on stage to recline barefooted on, I'd seriously give it a try.

July 21. None of my grandchildren will sleep with me when they visit. Michael told me, "You sleep too loud, Grandma."

Bob said, "It's called snoring, Michael."

July 22. My closet is badly in need of a sorting out and throwing away day. It is crammed full of clothes. Most of them are from the jitterbug era and are a size ten. I can't seem to part with them, even though I'll never be a size ten again and slow dancing is more my style these days.

Clothes are so expensive now. Bob needed some undershirts and I told him I'd found some in a catalog that were four for $3.52. He said, "Great, order me eight." Then I had to admit the catalog was from the year 1960. If he would be willing to wear poodles on his undershirts, I could make him some out of my old, felt jitterbug skirts embossed with poodles.

July 23. Bob wears a hearing aid, but he removes it when he comes home. I feel there's a message for me there somewhere.

July 24. I found a perfect, blue robin's egg lying in the street today. I carefully picked it up, brought it into the house, and laid it in a nest among the white eggs our dove, Cuckoo, has laid over the years.

I showed it to Bob and he said, "Have you blown it out, so it won't get smelly and rotten?"

I said, "Not me. I have no idea where that egg has been."

July 25. Some things are best left unsaid. I feel so good when the doctor says, "You're in good shape." Then I want to strangle him with his stethoscope when he adds, "for your age."

July 26. My ironing board was a source of amazement for one of my grandchildren, who asked me what it was for. I'm not going to say which grandchild. I'll just let my kids chew on that one for a while.

July 27. Do you know someone who has little annoy-ing habits that drive you up a tree? Someone close to me never pushes a chair back when he gets up from the table and he hangs up towels he uses inside out. He's very fortunate that I have no annoying habits that irritate him.

July 28. Bob and I went to Robin's graduation from college in Kearney, Nebraska, today. We're very proud of her. She received her Master of Arts degree in Education with an endorsement for Special Education-Learning Disabilities and it only took her nineteen years to earn it after she'd gotten her Bachelor of Arts degree.

July 29. My neighbor dropped in the other day while I was typing and asked me what I was doing. I said, "Writing kind of a book."

She asked me what kind of a book I was writing.

I said, "Kind of a 'Poor Erma Bombeck's Almanac'."

July 30. Kathy and Brent, our neighbors, have two dogs who are allowed in the house. Brent considerately made a doggy door for Patches, the bulldog and Marcus, the poodle, so they could come and go as they pleased, without disturbing the rest of the household.

All went well, until Kathy came home one day to find five dogs romping through their house and not one of the dogs belonged to them. Thank goodness Brent had installed the doggy door because every one of the dogs knew exactly where to exit when they realized they were unwelcome.

July 31. Bob likes to take a short nap after lunch. When he is working at the farm, he naps in the back of a truck and uses an empty bleach bottle covered with an old jacket for a pillow.

This makes me wonder why then, at home, his sleeping pillow must be only three inches thick with flexibility to double over at the ends.

August

August 1. It's a myth that older people are set in their ways. We've merely lived long enough to put some organization into our lives. There's a right way and a wrong way to do things, and ours just happens to always be the right way.

August 2. Pat is making another quilt. She bought a lovely piece of chambray for the basic color, but when she laid it out, she decided it was too nice to put in the quilt. Instead, she decided to save it to make a chambray dress or skirt. Her solution for the quilt pieces was to look in her closet, and lo and behold, what did she find there but a chambray skirt which she proceeded to cut up for the quilt.

The quilt is progressing beautifully, but I think I may install a lock on my closet in case Pat comes calling in search of more quilting material.

August 3. Speaking of material, the older you get, the more your skin begins to resemble crepe. Mine has gone past crepe and is fast approaching seersucker.

August 4. We don't care to travel a lot. Bob and I feel that if we can't get somewhere in half an hour, we probably don't need to go in the first place.

Our car is almost fifteen years old, and the mileage reads 58,505.7. It begs for retirement, but we tell it, "Not yet. We've got fifty years on you and a lot more mileage."

August 5. I've done extensive research on losing weight and my findings have been invaluable to me. I've learned never to buy a scale solely for the way it blends with your decoration scheme. Try them all in the store and get the one that registers the least pounds. Also, if you place the scale on carpet, you'll weigh four pounds less than you weigh on the same scale on a hard surface floor. It's also advisable to give the scale a good shake now and then.

August 6. Our white dove has laid 66 eggs, so far. She's three years old and kept us guessing as to what sex she was and we're still not sure. Cuckoo was six weeks old when I brought her home. I was told that only the male doves laugh. I was also assured I'd acquired a male because of the identifying dark gray ring of feathers around her neck. We waited patiently and five and a half months later Cuckoo laughed. "It's a boy," we proudly announced. One month later, Cuckoo laid her first egg. Go figure.

August 7. I wonder who has the contract to pick up all the used rubber from flat tires left lying around for motorists to dodge on the interstate highway. They must be very wealthy by now. Just imagine how many rubber soles for sneakers could be recycled out of only one day's haul.

August 8. Bob and I are incompatible in bed. I read — he doesn't. I snore — he doesn't. He's a light sleeper — I'm not. I like a fat pillow — he doesn't. He likes blanket sheets — I don't. When I'm cold — he's hot. When I'm hot — he's cold. Makes you wonder, doesn't it?

August 9. We went to Cozad, Nebraska, last Sunday to meet Kevin and Brandon. We brought Brandon home with us for his yearly summer visit. He celebrated his tenth birthday on July 28th and, like his dad, dearly loves motor sports and football games.

Although, he did catch my author fever while he was visiting us. His first effort was titled "Ten Stupid Laws." It included such wisdoms as "An elephant can't live in a lampshade." He also taught me how to use correction fluid, which is a miracle for typists like me, who make occasional mistakes.

August 10. I get irritated when I hear the comment "I bet she was a looker in her day." It always sounds like one's day is gone as soon as one is past the age of thirty. I don't think so. I think there's beauty in all ages.

August 11. I have an ingrown toenail. A year ago, while Michael was visiting, I took him to my doctor to have surgery on an ingrown toenail he was suffering with. I like a doctor with a good bedside manner and a touch of humor tossed in, if it's appropriate. Michael was a little concerned about my choice of a doctor when surgery began. The doctor's first words were, "Nurse, bring me a gallon bucket to catch the blood."

August 12. I just read an ad for a guaranteed 100-year nightlight. If I bought one, who could I will it to in order to make sure the guarantee would be honored in case it quit before the 100 years were over?

August 13. Reading our horoscopes today, I learned that my day will be filled with confusion. Then I hunted for Bob's horoscope to discover that they'd omitted his altogether. My horoscope was right. I'm already confused.

August 14. Remodeling is usually a nerve-wracking time. Our carpenter, Bob A., has made it a pleasure. He's been sprucing up our home for the past month and has become a friend, though this may just be my opinion. One day I asked him if he'd do yet another bit of repair, and because it was a very hot day, I told him not to work if the weather became unbearable. He said, "I have to keep working and get this job done soon—before you think of anything more for me to do."

On the other hand, I think he may be beginning to look upon me as a friend. I'm always borrowing his ladder to do some small chore and he promised to leave it to me in his will.

August 15. I really get annoyed with these telephone recordings you get when you call business firms. I called our insurance company and it went like this.

"Thank you for calling. If you wish to speak to accounting, press one. If you wish to speak to complaints, press two. If you wish to speak to policies, press three."

I pressed three.

"Thank you for calling. Our operators are all busy at this time. Please hold the line."

I held, through the entire musical score of "Annie Get Your Gun."

"Thank you for calling. If you wish to speak to accounting, press one. If you wish to speak to complaints, press two. If you wish to speak to policies, press three."

I pressed three.

"Hello. May I help you?"

I said, "At last, a human voice."

He laughed and said, "I'm sorry. This is a recording."

August 16. Wouldn't it be great if someone would invent a way for shorter people to reach the upper shelf in cupboards? Instead of a stepstool that's always in the way, or waiting for a tall person to walk by, there should be a button to push that would lower the cupboard to within our reach.

August 17. Our home is overrun with busy men today. There are two carpenters, five furnace and air conditioner men, two refrigerator men and Bob is running around somewhere. They're all wearing baseball caps. Throughout the day, I've learned to identify them by their cap logos. I guess making a statement on your cap is a male thing.

August 18. Our carpenter, Bob A., went to the doctor to have a benign tumor removed from his back. He asked the doctor where tumors come from. The doctor told him they were in his genes. Bob A. said, "They can't be. I wear bib overalls."

August 19. Age is a matter of mind. That's almost right. Age is a matter of mind over matter. When your body starts to go with the pull of gravity and you don't mind, that's when age becomes a matter of mind over matter.

August 20. I used to say my eyes were bigger than my stomach. That's no longer true. After years of believing that if I didn't clean my plate some poor child in a faraway land was going to starve, my stomach has finally grown larger than my eyes.

August 21. I'm finally done with the painting in the house that I started weeks ago. I usually get more paint on myself than I do on the walls, and this venture was no different. I don't know whether to discard my paint clothes or to make a modern art wall sculpture out of them. Maybe I'll make a floor lamp out of them because they're stiff enough to stand on their own.

August 22. Pat's back to her daily routine after her youngest son's wedding. Her youngest grandson Tim, who's five years old, was the ringbearer. To have him stand in the right spot, Father Joe placed a quarter on the floor and told him if he stood on that, he could keep the quarter after the ceremony practice. It went well, so Father Joe told him that's he'd put another quarter on the floor during the actual ceremony and if he did as well then, he could keep that quarter, too.

Tim looked at him, held up three fingers and said, "Three quarters."

Is Grandpa Willie teaching Tim these invaluable lessons of life?

August 23. Bob is a board person. He was on the Soil Conservation and Natural Resources District Board for six years. He was on the ASCS Board, which is an agricultural board, off and on for twenty years. He was on the Big Springs School Board for eight years. He was on the Farmers Elevator Board for nine years. He's currently serving his fourth term, which will be sixteen years when this term is over, as Deuel county commissioner of the Big Springs District. When he finally does retire, he'll really be a bored person.

August 24. I have a standard line I use when I get lost while driving, unlike men, who refuse to admit they are lost and keep driving around aimlessly. I explain it by saying, "I know where I'm going. I just thought we'd take the scenic route this time."

August 25. School starts today. Or is it football? Sometimes it's difficult to tell where one ends and the other begins. Each student has his own books, pencils and paper, and you don't see anyone fighting over possession of these things. I've always thought if they'd give each football player his own football, they wouldn't have to go out on a field in front of everyone and fight over one ball.

August 26. Margaret, Pat, and I went garage sale saleing today. We're good. We covered three garage sales, an antique auction, and Faber's hardware store's grand opening in less than two hours. I came home with a new pair of shoes, a slightly worn dress, a small wicker basket and something pretty that I haven't quite figured out what it is. This was all acquired for the unbelievable sum of nine dollars and ten cents.

August 27. I had to fill out a health questionnaire and was confused by one of the questions. They wanted to know if my husband's spouse was actively employed or retired. I looked for a third choice, but there was none. I consider myself active, but I don't get paid, so I guess I'm not actively employed, but I'm definitely not retired. Where was the choice for the housewife, mother, grandmother, or just plain busy person. I left the answer blank on that one. Let them figure it out.

August 28. Our friends' gardens have flourished this year. Bob A. brought us cucumbers, corn, beets, carrots, and zucchini. Pat and Willie gave us corn. Norma and John gave us corn and tomatoes. I dread the day that will surely come when they tell us we have our own dirt and it's time for us to start growing our own food.

August 29. I actually have a garden this year. It's a ten-inch pot of basil that I'm very proud of. I've been harvesting it for several weeks, and put it in almost everything I cook. I've learned that it looks pretty in everything, but it's an herb that doesn't enhance the flavor of all foods. For instance, I've discovered it does nothing for tapioca pudding.

August 30. When Bob and I were married, I brought a player piano with me into the marriage. Five years into our marriage, we had a carpet but no vacuum sweeper. I traded the piano for a sweeper.

Now I wish I'd kept the player piano and lived with dirty floors. As we mature, the "I wish I would haves" really pile up, don't they?

August 31. Pat and I went to Ogallala today and I found the perfect necklace and earrings to go with the slightly worn dress that I bought at the garage sale a week ago. Now I need new shoes and hose to match, a longer slip and my old coat really clashes with the color of the dress. Sometimes, my logic on saving money escapes even me.

September 1. When Robin was three years old and Kevin was just a baby, Bob bought a beautiful Arabian horse at a farm sale. She was named Ginger and because she was very gentle with children he felt that buying her would be a good investment. The only thing he didn't know at the time, was that Ginger didn't like adults on her back and since Bob also planned to ride her to bring in the cattle at night, this proved to be a problem. I'd look out the kitchen window to see Bob and Ginger bonding in the corral, going around circles with Bob begging, "Whoa. Whoa. C'mon, Ginger, whoa."

The result was that we finally sold Ginger and every time Robin asked where she was, we told her that Ginger was getting fitted for a new saddle. Five years later, we felt she was finally old enough to handle the truth, so we had to confess.

September 2. Opposites do attract. Bob is a true pessimist and I'm a steadfast optimist. He always smells the milk for his cereal every morning, expecting it to be sour. I taste it, sure it will be sweet. Once in a while, I'm wrong.

September 3. Today is our forty-seventh wedding anniversary and they said it wouldn't last. We were both nineteen years old when we married, and we literally grew up together. We're so accustomed to each other, we sometimes finish each other's sentences. I have to admit that I'm beginning to wonder if this is a positive thing or just an irritating habit. Will we make it to our forty-eighth wedding anniversary or will we finish each other's sentences just one too many times?

September 4. Why do husbands insist on saving all their old electric razors that will never cut a whisker again? Is it akin to wives who hoard old lipstick tubes that have run out of lipstick?

September 5. I finished my Christmas shopping today. I know, I can hear the groans. If I get it done early, I can tell myself that I'm saving money because prices are always going up.

I'll admit that I've never been able to fulfill Bob's Christmas wish. Every year he asks for a million dollars and a train load of spending money. Every year he is disappointed. If he did ever receive this gift, though, it wouldn't leave him anything to wish for the next year, would it?

September 6. I worry about very intelligent people. Are they lonely? Who do they talk with?

September 7. A great revelation has come to me. Reading back through what I've written, I've discovered that my mind wanders. This probably is the reason I never became a rocket scientist or a genetic engineer or a neurosurgeon or a conductor of symphonies. See, there it goes again.

September 8. Exercise is good. Today, I awoke to a beautiful day. The birds were singing and the weather was perfect, so I opened all the windows to let the outside in. Then the wind started to blow, the birds stopped singing, and the sky grew cloudy, so I closed all the windows to keep the outside out. That's enough exercise for one day.

September 9. Husbands improvise with grocery lists. I gave Bob a grocery list that had body deodorant written on it. He came home with a bottle of room deodorizer. Now that I reflect on it, maybe my problem was a lot bigger than I thought it was.

September 10. Everything about growing old isn't as good as it seems. Although your vocabulary does increase as you learn new words like triglycerides, cholesterol, osteoarthritis, osteoporosis, degeneration, and incontinuity. These are words I could have happily lived the rest of my life without learning.

September 11. Funerals are an unpleasant fact of life. Recently at a funeral, two sweet elderly ladies, who evidently made funerals a social event, were seated behind me. They weren't quite sure who was being laid to rest on that day, but they were quite certain about exactly what was served for the lunches at all the previous funerals they'd attended. I don't know if they kept notes, but I do know that the tuna casserole was much better at Herman's funeral than it was at Rudy's.

September 12. Bob lost his glasses the first day of the wheat harvest that has been over for a couple of months now. After scouring the entire countryside, a miracle has occurred. The elevator called to tell us someone has found them. We are very grateful. I had envisioned someone opening a loaf of bread somewhere, someday to find a pair of horn-rimmed glasses neatly sliced inside.

September 13. Thanks to our friends, Bob and I won't suffer this year from whatever it is one suffers with if one doesn't eat enough vegetables. They continue to give, bless them. Added to our hoard are tomatoes and peppers from Margaret; zucchini and peppers from Jean; tomatoes and peppers from Norma; cucumbers, carrots and beets from Bob A.; and rhubarb from Pat and Willie. We now have enough to set up our own roadside stand.

September 14. I guess we all have our quirky little habits. Bob not only sorts the paper money in his wallet by denomination, he also places the presidents right side up, all facing in the same direction.

This is the same person who also hangs his clothes up every night, carefully. Carefully tossed over the back of a chair, that is.

September 15. LaRae stopped by for a visit this afternoon. We sat on the front porch and had an in-depth discussion on world affairs and the problems with kids today. LaRae is ten years old.

September 16. Grass-mowing season is finally nearing an end for this year. Think how rich the person would be who could discover real grass that never grows more than two inches high.

September 17. Where does all the red tape come from? The older we get, we seem to have more and more forms to fill out that seem to become more and more difficult. We have insurance forms, social security forms, farm production forms, tax forms, and survey forms piled up to answer.

To help us retain our sanity through all this, I think we should start a red tape support group. To achieve this goal, I'd be willing to send out the forms to anyone interested in joining this cause.

September 18. Bob smugly said, "If I tried, I'll bet I couldn't do that again in a hundred years."

What did he do? Well, I had lunch ready on the table and Bob threw the ball for Killer. It hit the chair, bounced on the table, bounced over a fruit salad, bounced over the mashed potatoes, bounced over his place setting, and into a bowl of sliced cucumbers.

All I can say is "He better not try to do it again."

September 19. My dad taught me how to drive fifty years ago—long before the first drivers education class was held. He was a mechanic and insisted I learn all the parts on a car before I was even allowed behind the wheel of the family car.

Dad would be glad to know I actually retained some of his teaching. I remember where the steering wheel and ignition are, and so far, that's been enough to get me wherever I need to go.

September 20. Typewriter ribbon isn't an easy purchase. I went to Ogallala, Nebraska, and visited two discount stores, a variety store, two office supply stores, and the newspaper office. They all advised me to buy a new typewriter but I feel that would be a foolish waste of money. My typewriter is only twenty-nine years old.

Later, I went to Julesburg, Colorado, and located the necessary typewriter ribbon at their variety store. I bought two spools, just in case I run into this problem again within the next five years.

September 21. Wieners and hot dog buns never come out even. There are either two wieners left over, or two hot dog buns left over. I suspect that the meat packing companies and the bakeries have done this on purpose to perpetuate the continuous sale of these products.

September 22. This is Big Springs Day. Our town goes all out for this. We don't have to cook at home at all today, if we take in the rolls and coffee served in morning, sandwiches and Mexican food at noon, and the chili supper in the evening.

There are also booths with more food and arts and crafts. In the afternoon, there's a big parade with kids' games afterward and free ice cream. It's all capped off in the evening with the football game and the crowning of the high school homecoming royalty and the announcement of the parade float winners.

Pat, Margaret, Doris, and I have discovered our interest leans toward the food. Pat and I started at 8:00 in the morning with coffee and rolls at the Fire Hall and Margaret and Doris joined us at the Memorial Hall for more coffee and rolls. At noon, it was back to the Fire Hall for a lunch of barbecued beef sandwiches, baked beans, coleslaw, and pie. After the parade, we returned to the Memorial Hall for free ice cream sundaes. Some of us ordered burritos and pepper bellies to take home for our supper and some of us went back to the Fire Hall for the chili supper. It's been a very full day—in more ways than one. We'll wait until tomorrow to worry about all the extra calories we inhaled today.

September 23. Crickets are omens of good luck so I do not allow anyone to kill a cricket in our home. I make them carefully carry the cricket outdoors and set it free.

There was a cricket in our bathroom so, armed with a paper cup to transport him outdoors, I took pursuit. After a ten-minute chase, he took a hop, I took a step—crunch!

I really feel terrible. Will Jiminy Cricket ever forgive me?

September 24. I owe our son, Kevin, an apology. When he was four years old, he colored a picture on the wall in his room and was reprimanded for it. The second time, he colored a picture on the wall in the hall and he got a spanking.

A few weeks ago, our daughter Robin, who is forty-two years old and who was seven years old at the time of the coloring incident, admitted that the drawing on the wall in the hall was her work of art and not Kevin's.

So Kevin, I'm sorry and if it makes you feel any better, your sister has been severely reprimanded for her misconduct.

September 25. The Phelps Hotel is a one-hundred-eleven-year-old hotel in Big Springs that has been renovated and turned into a lovely historical bed and breakfast inn. Pat, Doris, Elaine, and I went to the grand opening.

There was a drawing for a beautiful, hand crocheted afghan that could be won by guessing the number of stitches it took to make it. I guessed 8,998 stitches and only missed winning it by 8,590 stitches.

September 26. I'm so proud of myself. Our furnace quit running so I called our furnace man. He told me what to do via a long-distance telephone call and I fixed it. It isn't relevant that I put the furnace door on wrong when I replaced the filter and caused it to quit in the first place.

September 27. Well, so much for my goal of losing a pound in the next three days. Doris and I went out for lunch today. We only ordered a ground sirloin sandwich, but it came with cheese, bacon, peppers, onions, and mushrooms on it, with a side order of French fries.

Earlier today, I made a coconut pineapple pie with a new recipe, so I had to give that a taste test. This afternoon, Margaret came over and since I figured it would have been rude of me not to eat what I offered her, I had another piece of pie. The only thing I can say in my defense, is that everything was washed down with non-fattening black coffee.

September 28. Why do projects grow into mountains from the anthill idea you began with? I thought I'd surprise Bob when he came home from a three-day trip to Illinois and have the rock garden finished that he and I had talked about making since last spring. So I called Vince, our town's yard expert, and he did the digging, edging, and laid the plastic for me. Then he started filling the area with the crushed rock that Bob and I had purchased for this project. We'd underestimated a little because six bags of crushed rock barely covered the area we'd prepared.

When Bob came home, he was pleased the project was underway and went to Ogallala to buy ten more bags of crushed rock which we added to the rock garden. It still barely covered the area.

Then we discovered there was no more rock to be found in any of the nearby towns. In desperation, I called Charlene at our Country Supply Store and asked her if they had crushed rock. She said they didn't and I asked her if they had any big rocks they could crush for us.

I finally located a store in North Platte, Nebraska, which is seventy-five miles from Big Springs, that still had some crushed rock left. Tomorrow, we'll go get the twenty bags they have on hand.

September 29. We thought the rock garden was such a great idea when we started. We did finish it today, but from an idea for a project with an estimated budget of $30, it ended up costing us $219.37.

Also, I'm trying to decide whether or not to tell Bob that there may be a very slight possibility his muscle aches and pains may be due to the fact that in the last two days, he's lifted a total of three-quarters of a ton of rocks.

September 30. I wonder if my children will ever figure out that bribery works wonders. I was talking to Robin on the telephone and she told me that Jillian wouldn't take the medicine the doctor had given her for an earache because one of the side effects was a possibility of nausea. I said, "Let me talk to her."

A little talking and a small private bribe did the trick. Grandma's magic conquers again.

October

October 1. Many years ago, Bob and our neighbor Melvin went to a farm sale and jointly bought a boat with a trailer to haul it home for the huge sum of $10 each. The boat was unbelievably heavy. It was made of wood and looked, for all the world, like an overgrown mutant canoe.

One very rainy season, the lagoons on our farm were filled to overflowing. Bob decided it would be fun to take Robin and Kevin, who were eight and five years old respectively, for a boat ride in our largest lagoon. This lagoon was inhabited by several ducks who were also enjoying the rainy days.

So Bob, Robin, and Kevin climbed into the pickup, dragging the boat on its trailer behind them. I watched them from the farm yard. They seemed to be having a grand time when an official looking vehicle stopped on the road near the lagoon. Out stepped a tall, burly man wearing the uniform of a game warden. He waded through the mud to the lagoon and after a lengthy chat with Bob, retraced his steps and drove away.

When my family arrived back home, I asked Bob what the game warden wanted. He said, "You won't believe this, but he seriously wanted to know if I had a license to hunt those ducks."

October 2. Two of my favorite relatives, Walt and Shirley, stopped for a visit today. Walt, who is twelve years older than I, used to tease me unmercifully when I was a small child. He painted my doll's toenails, fingernails, and belly button with bright red nail polish. Then, he'd toss her off the porch say, "Want to see her dive, Betty?" I'd run to the doll's rescue, bring her back, and we'd go through the same ritual for hours on end.

Once he took me to a scary movie in a theatre that had a long hall with several doors opening into it. In the movie, all sorts of monsters kept jumping out of these doors. My grandparents' house also had a long hall with several doors opening into it. This was the perfect setting for my Uncle Walt to reenact the movie. I got the part of the frightened heroine, while he played the role of the monster lying in wait behind one of the doors. He'd hide, call my name, and I'd run down the hall. He'd jump out into the hall, scaring the living daylights out of me. He's still my favorite uncle, but I insist on sleeping with a nightlight on to this day.

Walt told me as they were leaving today that he's trying to talk a friend of his into shaving his dog to prove that under the black and white hair, his skin will be black. That the part that's Dalmatian; under the white hair, his skin will be white. And I thought age was a mellower. Luckily, Shirley has the patience of an angel and a good sense of humor.

October 3. We went to Lewellen, Nebraska, this evening for a long overdue visit with Harold and June whom we met many years ago on a rare night out and have remained friends since that first meeting.

June has more artistic talent in her little finger than I have in my whole hand. One year for my birthday she gave me a watercolor picture she had painted. It had won first place in an art show. It hangs on our dining room wall and is one of my most prized possessions.

On the other hand, one of Bob's most prized possessions is an Irish fly swatter Harold had made. He made it out of the plastic rings that hold a six-pack of pop together which is taped to one end of a window shade slat. I put a magnet on it, and it hangs on our refrigerator. I guess art is in the eye of the beholder.

October 4. I could put an "Open for business" sign on my closet and start a small boutique. It's already stocked with sizes ranging from "Twiggy" to "Dumbo."

October 5. My clothing needs are simple. I'm so sure I won't get caught in a heavy downpour of rain, a snowstorm, the desert, or a swimming pool that I don't own galoshes, snow boots, a sunbonnet, or a swimming suit.

October 6. Being an only child isn't all it's cracked up to be. For instance, I was an only child and I know how irritating life can be when you have no brothers or sisters to blame your misconduct on. When Kevin was a teenager, he was corrected for leaving the cap off the tube of toothpaste. The first words out of his mouth were an automatic, "Robin did it."

I said, "That won't fly, Kevin. Nice try, but Robin's away at college and hasn't been home for a month."

October 7. Our grandson, Michael, a high school senior, had the honor of being chosen as one of 190 high school musicians from across the state of Nebraska to march and play his saxophone in the Shrine Bowl All-Star High School Band for the parade and halftime at the Cornhusker football game in Lincoln, Nebraska.

The game was broadcast live on television and I tried to locate Michael at halftime. I must admit that I was getting very irate. While I was trying to see and hear my grandson, the announcers kept interrupting with something they called football information.

October 8. Do you remember when your life was scheduled around Monday night television? Not for Monday Night Football, but for something much more important—"Ben Casey."

On Tuesday morning, our partyline telephone was all abuzz with the details of the program from the night before. Margaret always had all the symptoms of the ailment on Tuesday morning that Dr. Ben Casey had cured on Monday night but, fortunately, she always recovered in time for the next episode.

October 9. One nice thing about growing older is I don't have to worry about a zit popping up on my nose before the prom dance.

October 10. Our daughter-in-law Mary is a whiz on computers. To me, a mouse is something you jump on a chair to avoid; software is a paper plate; and windows are things you open to air out the house. I'm sure she could clarify this for me but it would just be more knowledge for my brain to store and there's enough in there already to confuse me.

October 11. Doris and I rode to Sidney, Nebraska, with Pat this afternoon. Sidney is a little over ten times the size of Big Springs. We discovered that three senior citizens engaged in a lively conversation from a small town can cause cars to brake rapidly if they walk when the sign says "DON'T WALK."

October 12. I finally had my dental appointment this morning to get my broken tooth repaired. I've learned something about the value of self-worth. When I was born, I was worth free exchange labor from my dad and a bushel of sweet corn from my mom's garden. I was informed today by my dentist that just one tooth in my head is worth $440.

October 13. I'm enjoying a bowl of sliced peaches with cream. It reminded me of Robin and Jillian's visit last summer. While we were grocery shopping one day, Jillian spied some fresh Colorado peaches. I bought some and she was so excited about my purchase, that I asked her if they had never had fresh peaches in eastern Nebraska.

She said, "Yes, but not the good Colorado peaches."
I said, "What kind do they have?"
Jillian replied, "Generic."

October 14. I have to preface this by telling you that forty-odd years ago, there were five young married couples who spent a lot of their time together. Bob and I were among this group and Vance and Donna were one of the other couples. Sadly, Vance is no longer with us, but Donna is visiting Pat and Willie this weekend, so I walked over for coffee and a chat.

During the conversation, Bob's and my wedding was mentioned. Since Vance and Donna didn't meet until a few years after Bob and I were married, I told her that Vance sang at our wedding. She said, "I didn't know Vance was a singer."

I said, "He wasn't."

October 15. As I get older, I find I can't accomplish some of the physical tasks that I used to do easily when I was younger. It's frustrating but, on the other hand, my age also works as a plausible excuse for not doing the things I don't want to do anyway.

October 16. I just realized I'm 455 years old in dog years. No wonder the urge to fetch is gone.

October 17. Today is Bob's 66th birthday and he left this morning for Omaha, Nebraska, to attend a three day convention for the Nebraska Association of County Officials. In the thirteen years he's been a county commissioner, he's never attended the yearly convention, so he thought he should go once.

I don't know what I'm going to do while he's gone. He made me promise that I wouldn't start a major project for him to finish when he returns home.

October 18. The wind blew today with gusts of 45-miles an hour. A brand-new outdoor grill cover blew into our yard. I've been calling the neighbors trying to locate the owner—with no luck. Because we don't own a grill, I could have saved a lot of telephone time if the grill had blown into our yard, too—under the cover. Then we could have looked forward to eating outside next summer.

October 19. The grill cover blowing into our yard reminded me of the neighborhood block picnic that was held in Dayton and Virginia's yard last summer. The weather was beautiful. The food was delicious—it should have been. I figured that given the number of people attending and the number of years we've all been cooking, we had 750 years of experience among us.

There was even some unexpected entertainment. Elaine's plastic fork broke as she was spearing some food on her plate and her onion rings magically flew in circles across the entire length of the picnic table. Elaine watched their flight through the air and said, "Well, I've been trying to cut down on my eating anyway."

October 20. Bob came home this afternoon from the convention wearing a straw hat. Straw hat weather has been over for a couple of months now so I assumed I had better get my suitcase packed. Surely this means we're going to vacation in the Bahamas.

For right now, it's back to the kitchen after three days of loafing. How about if I said, "We have to eat out tonight. I seem to have forgotten how to cook." Do you think that would work? No, I don't think so either.

October 21. I have a tendency to eat things I like that Bob doesn't care for when he's not home. Between me and the stomach fairy, I learned while Bob was in Omaha that oyster stew, peanut butter toast, string cheese, and chocolate ice cream drenched in butterscotch syrup are not a compatible balanced meal.

October 22. The calendar has today marked as "Sweetest Day." Does anyone know what that's all about? Does it mean you can eat sweets all day? Or is everyone supposed to wear their sweetest smiles? Or is the weather to be pure and sweet? Or did some joker just put that on the calendar to confuse people like me?

October 23. Nostalgia is highly overrated. Does anyone really Want To Go Back to the days of the outhouses with flypaper curls hanging in your hair in the summer and cold catalogs in the winter?

October 24. Today is United Nations Day. How in the world can I hope for countries to agree on anything when my son and daughter can't? Although, when they were younger, they did share their chili soup. Robin didn't like meat, so she picked out the hamburger and gave it to Kevin. Kevin didn't like beans, so he picked them out and gave them to Robin. Maybe there's hope for the world after all.

October 25. Doris, Elaine, and I heard an offer we couldn't refuse. The second-hand store in Ogallala was having a half-price sale.

Doris bought four well-crammed bags of clothes for her ten grandchildren for $10.

Elaine emerged with two stuffed bags for $5 which included a pretty opal ring and a lacy black negligee. I wonder what her plans include.

I spent $4.40 and purchased one pair of jeans and three shirts for Bob and a pair of shorts, a blouse and a pair of purple earrings for myself.

We were so pleased with ourselves. When you're our age you see, it doesn't take a big win on the lottery to make your day.

October 26. I'm getting slightly forgetful as I grow older. I checked out *Insomnia* by Stephen King at the library today. I looked forward to reading it, so at bedtime I put on my nightgown, fluffed my pillow, and curled up to read. I discovered after rereading the first ninety-two pages that I'd read it before. Just last year, in fact.

With a grin, Michael always asks me what a book I've read was about, knowing all the while I have a short retention span and never remember much about a book once I close the cover. I'm sure that's because I feel living in the past is futile. I prefer to look ahead to reading the next book that I probably won't remember either.

October 27. Talking about being forgetful, Bob and I fretted and stewed all day trying to remember a lady's name that we both knew and neither could recall.

We went out for supper and upon leaving the restaurant saw a truck parked behind our car that prevented us from leaving. In huge block letters on the side of the truck was the word "GRACE." That was the lady's name. Bob and I looked at each other in astonishment. Laughing, I said, "Talk about a sign from the beyond."

October 28. Do you ever wonder what happened to people who made a deep impression on you in your past? I wonder what happened to Miss Hochstettler. She was my favorite high school teacher and she taught English and literature. Besides teaching me to love literature, she taught me another valuable lesson.

My high school boyfriend didn't like literature so when he asked me if I'd write his essay assignment for him, I did. He got an A+ on his paper. I got a B- on mine.

It took me a long time to realize she knew I'd done it for him and she hoped to get my attention by downgrading me. When it finally dawned on me, I learned that when you cheat, nobody wins. Someone always loses, whether you're the cheater or the cheatee.

October 29. Time to set our clocks back an hour and gain that hour back that we've been without since last spring. I'll bet the younger generation doesn't know that once upon a time, the time stayed the same all year long. It seems life was so much simpler then.

October 30. Raking leaves isn't my idea of fun. I never thought I could feel animosity toward a tree, but there's a tree in our neighborhood that I don't feel any kindness toward. It's a huge, old cottonwood who must have a dislike for us, too. I can almost hear it laughing as it drops most of its leaves into our yard every fall.

In the past eight years, I've threatened to go in the dark of night and cut it down, a small sliver at a time, so no one would notice when it had disappeared completely.

October 31. This year I kept our Halloween decorations to a minimum. Last year, I went all out and even went so far as to construct a "grave" in our front porch planter. I made a tombstone that said "Here lies Hal O'Ween." Then I went to our Family Market grocery store and asked Kevin for some extra large bones so I could build a half-buried skeleton. Do you know how hard it is to arrange cow bones so they look like a human skeleton? Anyway, I was really kind of pleased with the end result, until I awoke the next morning to discover that the dogs in the neighborhood liked it, too. My skeleton lost his thigh bone completely to the four-legged gravediggers, and I had to gather an arm bone from the front yard while his ribs were lying on the front steps. After reassembling him the best I could from the remaining bones, I sprayed him liberally with "Dog Off" and he rested in peace until Halloween was over.

November

November 1. Tonight is one of the bi-weekly drawings for the state and interstate lotteries. I keep reading in the newspapers, hearing on the radio, and watching on television about how unhappy the previous millionaire winners of the lotteries are. I'd like to win once and see how unhappy being a millionaire would make me.

November 2. Bob and I got our flu shots today. Bob got this kind, gentle, angelic nurse who smiled sweetly and patted his shoulder when he said, "Are you done? I didn't feel a thing." I got the nurse from hell. She gave my inoculation to me with a porcupine quill that was driven into my arm with a jackhammer.

The two nurses did have one thing in common. My nurse also smiled sweetly, when I winced in pain.

November 3. Today is Sam's eighth birthday. Sam and Brandon are definitely sales entrepreneurs. The last time they called, it was to sell Grandma some long-distance caramel popcorn for their school. After the usual chit-chat with them and Katie, Sam came back on the line and said, "Grandma, I'm also collecting money donations for a worthy cause."

Yes, of course, I bought and yes, of course, I donated. Grandmas are notoriously soft touches.

November 4. The clothes hamper is full, so it must be time to do the laundry. Do you remember when clothes were run through a wringer on the washing machine? It was usually a race with the wringer to see if you could pop it apart before it ate the buttons off your favorite blouse.

You always knew what you were going to be doing every Monday and Tuesday of the week. Monday, you washed laundry and hung it outside on the clothesline to dry. Summers were better for this because winters meant frozen clothes that you brought back into the house stacked like pancakes.

On Tuesdays, you ironed all day long so everyone would have nice, clean, crisp, fresh clothes to get dirty again. This meant that next Monday you could start the ritual all over again. By the time Tuesday evenings rolled around, I was ready to chuck the whole clothing idea and enroll our family in a nudist colony.

November 5. I've been thinking about the names they give colors these days.

Green isn't green. It's kiwi, celery, cucumber or avocado.

Red isn't red. It's cherry, watermelon, strawberry, or tomato.

Yellow isn't yellow. It's banana, lemon, or mango.

Orange isn't orange. It's pumpkin, cantaloupe, or apricot.

Purple isn't purple. It's plum, eggplant, or grape.

Blue isn't simply blue. It's blueberry.

Thank goodness for rust. It's clay or adobe. At least this stops the temptation to nibble on our clothes as we wear them.

November 6. When husbands retire, it doesn't follow that wives get to retire, too. Meal planning and cooking still consume a large part of wives' lives. Years ago, I made a recipe box that I still use. I embroidered the words "LET'S EAT—OUT!" on the front. These are words to live by if I could somehow get the message across to my other, better-eating half. I guess it's too subtle.

November 7. Today is Election Day. I'm excited because I get to vote on everything today. I'm a registered Independent which means when there are primary elections, I'm not allowed to vote on political issues. On primary election days, I feel like a banana peel that's been tossed aside, but today I feel more like a top banana.

November 8. I collect bells and now have 65. It's an enjoyable hobby, but I've discovered through the years that they get dusty and need to be cleaned periodically, so today I'm going to clean the bell cupboard. To prevent breakage, I think every ten years should be often enough, don't you?

November 9. The good old days weren't always so good, were they? The young couple, Andy and Julie, who bought our farm home are having sewer problems which reminded me of the "good old days" with the outhouse out back.

Summers were kind of nice because you could find some solitude there, just sitting and looking through what was left of last year's catalog.

Winters were a different story. It took at least ten minutes to make the journey. First, you had to put on galoshes, a coat, mittens, and a scarf but when you reached your destination, chattering teeth and cold air coming through the walls deterred all thought of reading and relaxing.

I always wondered why most of these little houses had two holes and sometimes three or four. I never thought of this outing as a family affair.

November 10. How about this for conning yourself into believing you're eating healthy? I fixed myself a lean lunch that consisted of a baked potato, broccoli, and cheese. Sounds smart, right? The problem was, it just didn't taste good until I slapped on a little salt, a couple tablespoons of butter and a couple of teaspoons of sour cream.

November 11. The carpet layers are replacing the badly worn carpet in our living room today. There's an invisible bond between working men and their radios. They may forget their tools but never their radios. It's also an unwritten rule that the radio needs to be tuned to an ear-splitting volume. This is probably good for their lungs, because when any sort of verbal communication is attempted, they have to take a deep breath in order to have enough air in their lungs to shout loud enough to be heard above the radio.

It's too loud for me. I can still hear it through my ear muffs.

November 12. Robin, Michael, and Jillian came this weekend for a visit. There was one small incident that made me wonder for an instant if they enjoyed the visit as much as I did.

I make the mistake of feeding Killer the same food as we humans are eating. I made meat loaf today for the noon meal and after we'd all eaten, I looked down at Killer's plate on the floor and commented on the fact that he hadn't touched his food at all. Then I said, "Now, I remember. The last time Killer ate my meat loaf, he was ill for two days afterward."

In the silence that followed, I looked around the table and realized I'd never seen people turn such delightful shades of green before.

November 13. I will never use another napkin ring without thinking of dogs. One time, when Bob and I picked up Sam in Lexington, Nebraska, for a visit with us, we stopped in North Platte on the way home to do a little shopping. I was looking for a new shower liner, while across the aisle Sam noticed the large variety of napkin rings that came in sets of four. "Look Grandma," he said, "bracelets for dogs."

November 14. According to talk shows and women's magazines, ladies are more likely than not to look in other peoples' bathroom medicine cabinets. This is one flaw I do not have and I have never ever considered that other people might be checking ours out. Therefore, I really don't keep it neat enough for close inspection. Maybe I'd better do something about that. I'll run down to the hardware store right now and buy a combination lock for it. That would be easier than cleaning it out, I think.

November 15. My friend Vy gave me a tip years ago that has made my life much easier. You know when you put pantyhose on how the crotch always seems to reach about mid-thigh? If you lower your body to a half-squat position, and then stand up they will miraculously fit just right. A little tug and you're on your way.

Don't attempt to adjust your pantyhose in this manner in public. I've gotten some strange looks from people when I tried it.

November 16. A new discount store has opened in Ogallala. Pat called and said, "Someone needs to check it out." We both wanted desperately to do our housework today but being the conscientious citizens we are, Pat and I will sacrifice our valuable time and check it out. We will then report our findings to those in our community who were unable to go.

November 17. I just returned home from another trip to the dentist. I'm suspicious of the fact that my dentist never stays in the room with me when I have x-rays taken. Also, the heavy lead bib he puts on me for my protection is a long way from my teeth. If all this is supposed to be comforting, it isn't.

Besides, if they're going to put a bib on you, shouldn't they at least serve you lobster or spaghetti?

November 18. When Kevin was about four years old, he hated riding in the car. We would barely get started for a ride when a small voice from the back seat was heard saying, "Are we there yet?" We always gave him the same answer, "Just over the next hill." This would satisfy him for a minute. Then the ritual was repeated every half hour until we arrived at our destination.

I just realized something. Some thirty-odd years later, Bob and I are still trying to get over the next hill.

November 19. Bob and I stuffed ourselves with pancakes and sausage this evening. The Big Springs Improvement Group, otherwise known as B.I.G., served a pancake feed at the Fire Hall with the proceeds going toward obtaining bleachers for the newly sodded baseball diamond.

I noticed most of our neighbors were there, too. At least, I won't worry that any of them are watching their diets better than we are tonight. Sausage, pancake stacks, lots of butter and gallons of maple syrup. I don't see anything in that menu that's skinny food. Oh well, we'll all chow down. After all, it's for a good cause.

November 20. The last telephone conversation I had with four-year-old Katie went like this.

"Grandma, I'm taking dance lessons."

"That's great, Katie. Are they fun?"

"Yes, but it's really hard."

I asked her what was hard about it.

Katie said, "The hardest part is you have to learn how to stand in a straight line."

Growing up is sometimes tough, isn't it?

November 21. Do you ever have one of those days that you know, right from the beginning isn't going to be one of your better days? I'm having one of those days today.

First of all, my day started much too early. Our basset hound Sophie began her day at 3:00 in the morning. When she was sure I was awake and couldn't get back to sleep, she resumed her sleeping.

I decided to make a pot of coffee. As I was removing the soggy coffee grounds from the coffee pot, they flew from my hands showering the wall, floor, countertop, and curtains with ugly stains.

After I got this mess cleaned up, I saw that the trash bag was overflowing, so I proceeded to tie it up to take it to the dumpster. Well, the tie-string broke and the trash in the bag was still overflowing except that it was now overflowing all over the floor.

After I cleaned up the trash and scrubbed the floor, I realized what the problem was. Today is Sunday. Supposedly a day of rest and that's just what I intend to do the rest of the day.

November 22. I made up a new word. Squill, meaning to be squeamish, squirrelly or swimmingly nauseous.

That is, I thought I made a new word. I looked in the dictionary to be sure and it was already there. It means a sea onion to be used as an expectorant, cardiac stimulant, or a diuretic.

I like my meaning better.

November 23. Today is Thanksgiving Day. I'm reminded of my first attempt at fixing Thanksgiving dinner for our relatives. Things turned out reasonably well until it was time to carve the turkey which I insisted Bob do at the dining table.

Everyone was quite impressed until Bob said, "What's this?" He then proceeded to pull a lumpy paper bag from inside the turkey.

"So that's where they hide the giblets!" I exclaimed.

This episode has made me paranoid. Nothing leaves my kitchen now without being sliced into thin pieces, just in case there may be other things hidden inside of something else.

November 24. Imaginary friends are an absolute must in a happy childhood. Robin and Kevin each had one of their own.

Robin's friend was Judy. One day we were going for a ride in the car and as Robin crawled into the back seat, she immediately started sobbing uncontrollably. I asked her what was wrong. She cried, "Mom, you shut Judy in the car door." So I got out and opened the car door so Judy could climb inside to sit beside Robin.

Kevin's friend was Max and he lived in the dog house. Kevin spent hours in the dog house playing with Max. Sometimes, Max's family came to visit and they'd have parties in the dog house. On those days, Dude the dog usually got evicted.

November 25. Senior citizens like to compare their childhoods. The more deprived you were as a child, the higher your standing becomes in the group.

At what age you were, when you finally acquired running water in the home is a biggy. Also, whoever was the last one to take a bath in the same water as the rest of the family raises your ratings immensely. Whoever has the best reason for using the outhouse as an excuse to get out of doing a chore ranks right up there. I won the contest for who had the farthest to walk to school.

November 26. When Bob was in the United States Air Force, all his buddies had pin-up pictures of their girlfriends or wives. Not wanting to shirk my duty to my man and my country, I sent Bob a picture of me. I put on a huge fake nose, a large pair of horn-rimmed glasses, and an old pair of my Dad's work shoes. My Mom took a great close-up picture of me in a seductive pose on the porch.

If he ever showed it to anyone else, I never knew. Probably not, unless he was making a play for sympathy.

November 27. To escape the noise and worries of the world and his wife and two children, Bob used to hop in his Cessna 120 and fly away from it all. Because of the noise and worries of the world and his wife and two children, Bob eventually parted with his beloved airplane. He's found another solution for escape from the cares of the universe to replace flying. He simply removes his hearing aid.

November 28. When we're young, we become obsessed with a part of our anatomy that we feel is in need of changing. Mine was my nose. I hungered for a cute, turned up nose like my Mother's, but I'd inherited my longer nose from my Dad.

I spent hours pushing the tip of my nose up with my finger in the hope of reshaping it to perfection. I'd fall asleep at night in that position, with the idea that I would awaken in the morning with my ideal nose. One night, I even went so far as to adhesive tape my finger to my nose, so it wouldn't slide off as soon as I fell asleep. That lasted for about five seconds, as soon as I discovered I couldn't breathe through the tape. As my Mother cut the tape off my nose, she told me I was going to end up looking like a pig if I didn't stop the foolishness.

After breaking my nose twice, once when I was six and fell off the seesaw at school, and once again when I was eight and ran into a tree, I finally decided it was time to give up my quest for beauty.

Now, between the wrinkles and the bags under my eyes, I hardly notice my nose isn't perfect anymore.

November 29. Pat and I seem to wear similar outfits at the same time, without any consultation. Today we wore gray sweatshirts, black slacks, and red sweaters. Pat said, "Well, they say great minds run in the same direction, but so does dirty dishwater."

November 30. Bob has a fantasy. When his ship comes in, he wants to take a six-month ocean cruise around the world on it.

When we lived in the Panama Canal Zone for three years, during Bob's stint in the United States Air Force, I used to get seasick every time we waited for the ferry to transport us across the canal. This happened while we were still on dry land. When we actually boarded the ferry, it was touch and go, as to whether I'd be able to keep my lunch intact or not.

As you can see, I think Bob will have to go on an ocean voyage without me. Of course, as he says, when his ship comes in, he'll probably be at the airport.

December

December 1. I decided to do something different with the Christmas tree this year. Instead of dragging out the ornaments and trim, I trimmed it with lots of colored lights and 252 candy canes. There's some logic behind this. I figure the children, young and old, can eat the candy canes and untrim the tree for me at the same time.

December 2. Margaret, Pat, Doris, and I took in the Christmas Craft Fair at the Memorial Hall today. There were twenty tables, with local and surrounding areas represented. There are lots of crafty people around here, especially the crafty person overseeing the table where a wall hanging caught my eye. It was the perfect color, price, and decor to replace the old one hanging on our wall now, so naturally, I snatched it up right away. Well, when I got home, I hung it on the wall to discover it was sewn so crooked I had to tilt my head sideways to look at it. Now, I have to take it all apart and resew it. The old wall hanging is starting to look real good to me.

December 3. Kindness can kill. I thought I'd be nice to my house plants and feed them some fertilizer. I overdid a good thing. some of them gave a last gasp, folded their leaves, and left this world for plant heaven. So much for good deeds. I would've been a failure as a Boy Scout.

December 4. Today I'll address Christmas cards and write a short note in some of them to friends and relatives, whom we seem to keep in touch with only during the holiday season.

Some Christmas cards are only sent every other year. I forget to send a card to someone one year and we get one from them, so the next year, I send them a card and they don't send us one. It goes back and forth like that and through the years, I've probably saved $20 just by not sending that one card every year. Look how much I could save, if I didn't send any at all. But then, what could I tape on my kitchen cupboards at Christmas time to cover the grease spots?

December 5. This day isn't off to a good start. I awoke this morning at 3:30 A.M., thinking I'd forgotten to write eggs on the grocery list. It kept me awake, so at 4:00 A.M., I got up to write eggs on the grocery list, only to discover I'd already written it down. By then, sleep was out of the question for a while, so I decided to make some snacks for the holidays. I settled on "Puppy Chow," which is simple enough to make and consists of melting chocolate chips, butter, and peanut butter together. Then a box of cereal is stirred into the mixture and poured into a bag of powdered sugar. This is shaken well, and it's all done with ease. I was wrong.

To begin with, I had bought all natural peanut butter, which is nothing more than a hard layer of crushed peanuts with oil poured on top. This, you are supposed to be able to stir together. It doesn't work. As soon as I started to stir, a huge glob of oil shot out of the jar and oozed all over my sleeve. That should've been a clue, but I kept going.

I'd put the powdered sugar in a zippered plastic bag, thinking that was a clever idea. After I had the mixture poured into the bag, I started shaking it vigorously, only to find that I hadn't zipped it shut. One good shake, and a good portion of "Puppy Chow" went on the floor. Killer came running over to check it out, sniffed it, and walked away, leaving it for me to clean up.

Still not having reached the conclusion that this wasn't going to be a great day, I decided to make a batch of cookies which called for a cup of softened butter. I opened the pound of butter, unwrapped two sticks, put the wrappers back in the refrigerator, and threw the butter in the trash bin. Okay, I've finally gotten the hint. I'm going back to bed. Wake me when tomorrow gets here.

December 6. Christmas is fast approaching. It took two years for one of my Christmas gifts to become one of my favorite memories. Bob gave me a beautiful red dress one year that didn't fit, so I sadly returned it. The next Christmas, I unwrapped my present from Bob and couldn't believe my eyes. He'd given me the same beautiful red dress that he'd given me the year before. I said, "Thank you, honey. I really like this dress, and I can tell you really like this dress, but I'm afraid it isn't going to fit any better this year than it did last year."

December 7. It gets harder to trim your toenails as you grow older. I used to be able to sit in comfort on a chair, put my foot in my lap and trim my toenails with ease. Now, I've had to find a chair just the right height to put my foot on and bend over to do my pedicure. This chair can't be so high that I can't get my leg up on it, nor so low that I can't bend over that far without toppling over. I've found that the bathroom stool is the perfect height for this procedure.

December 8. It's a raw, blustery, wintry day. The temperature is three degrees above zero, but the wind is blowing so hard, the wind chill index is forty-five degrees below zero.

Our yard has garnered a couple of red Christmas outdoor decoration bows. Our bow has also blown away, but the ones that blew in are much nicer. I owe someone in our neighborhood a thank you note.

December 9. Everyone has a collection of things they feel they're being frivolous with if they throw them away. Mine is leftover holiday cards form Easter, Valentine's Day, Halloween and Christmas. Lately, I decided they were piling up, so I started doing my correspondence with them. Last week, I wrote Robin a short letter on a Valentine card. She said a friend of hers asked her if her mother was early or late. Robin said, "Neither. That's my mother's idea of conservation."

December 10. The Publisher's Clearing House was scheduled to stop here yesterday. I had the ice bucket ready for the champagne they bring, a vase filled with water for the flowers they bring, the welcome mat was swept, our camera had a new roll of film in it, my hair was combed, and the lighting was perfect for the film crew. Can you believe this? They never showed up. They'll be sorry they missed the nine-course meal I also had catered for them.

December 11. I hate these child-proof pill bottle caps. In the time it takes for me to open them, I could've hunted for a child to open the bottle for me, and have recovered from whatever I needed the pill for in the first place.

December 12. I've broken the habit I'd acquired of drinking a bottle of pop daily. I've started drinking water instead. I'm seriously thinking of going back to drinking pop. Water has no taste and it's fattening. I've gained two pounds.

December 13. I used to be so gullible when it came to believing everything anyone said or everything I read. I once bought a weight-reducing apparatus which consisted of a plastic pair of trousers with a flexible hose attached on the side. The hose was attached to the vacuum sweeper, which you turned on and went about your daily chores. Of course, this procedure ballooned the trousers and the sweeper trailed along beside you, so it was difficult to do any chores. This agenda was to be done for three hours daily, until the desired weight loss was attained.

I dreaded the times when someone would drop by for a visit. It was embarrassing to have anyone see me rigged up like that. I looked like an elephant taking a pet armadillo for a walk.

Needless to say, I never lost an ounce in that outfit.

December 14. Life is like a gourmet meal.

Youth is the appetizer, eager for what lies ahead.

The teen years are the soup and salad days, carefree and light, with the main course just around the corner.

Adulthood is the entree. Meat and potatoes, the productive years.

Middle age is the dessert. A time to look around and enjoy the sweetness of the productive years.

Senior citizenry is the fine wine. A time to reflect and savor each sip of life every day in every way.

December 15. As we grow older, our hair tends to grow thinner. The new rage in our area is washing your hair with horse shampoo. Everyone around here sings praises for it, so I finally decided to try it. After all, has anyone ever seen a bald horse?

There's a slight side effect that's hardly noticeable. When someone asks me a question with the answer being a number, I tend to neigh and stomp my foot to answer.

December 16. Some of the families in and around Big Springs are gracious enough at Christmas time to open their home to the public for tours to see their lovely decorations for the holiday season. Pat chauffeured a carload of us around to visit the homes on the tour.

One of the homeowners had a brilliant idea, that I intend to put to use year-round on our basement door. She'd tied her laundry room door up like a Christmas package with a huge ribbon and a large tag that read "Do Not Open 'Til Christmas."

December 17. Quitting a bad habit cold turkey isn't a good idea. I crave chocolate stars, morning, noon, and night, and am trying to stop. I get no help from the chocolate stars, either. Every time I shop and get to the check-out counter, I find a bag of chocolate stars has jumped from the store shelf right into my grocery cart. I don't like to hold up the checkout line, so I can't return them to the shelf. I'm stuck with taking them home with me. Once I'm home, after a time, I notice they're taking up valuable space in the cupboard and, as it is left to me to solve this problem, the only thing to do is to get rid of them. Not wanting to be wasteful, I can't just throw them away. The only other choice I have, is to eat them. After savoring the taste of one luscious melting star, I'm hooked again. Chocolate withdrawal is not a pretty sight.

December 18. Our dove, Cuckoo, just laid her 77th egg. Birds have an easier way of giving birth than humans do. Just think how much easier it would be to just lay an egg and sit around on it, waiting for a beautiful baby to bounce out, while your husband did the household chores and brought all your meals to you in bed, like the male birds do for their mates. I don't think I could get used to a female bird's way of eating secondhand food, though.

December 19. The tank lever broke on our bathroom toilet, but Bob has fixed it. He attached a fly swatter to the chain pull. To flush the toilet, all we need to do is pull on the fly swatter.

It actually works, and is such a novel idea, that we may leave it that way, for a conversation topic.

December 20. Today is Kevin's birthday. He was an early Christmas present for Bob and me thirty-eight years ago. He's a manager of a concrete plant in Silver Creek, Nebraska.

I wish all our children and grandchildren lived closer to us. I miss Kevin's sense of humor and I admire his honesty. Whereas, I sometimes hedge on opinions, Kevin tells it like he sees it. I have to admit though, he's probably much too honest to be a good used car salesman or a politician.

December 21. Kevin has inherited a personality trait from me that I'm not particularly proud of. Neither of us forgives easily. Now that I comprehend that much, I understand his reaction during one event a little better than I did at the time it happened.

When Kevin was five years old, he hid from us, fearing a reprimand for some minor infraction. When you live on a farm and can't find your child, it's time to panic. Bob, Robin, and I hunted and called his name for two long hours. Robin found him hiding behind the lilac bush hedge, and yelled out, "Here he is."

He did get a spanking, not for whatever it was he had done, but for hiding and scaring us so badly. Anyway, I don't think to this day that Kevin has forgiven Robin for telling on him.

December 22. Today a salesman called trying to sell us new siding for our home. I said, "No."

Then he tried to sell us new windows. I said, "No."

Next came cupboards. I said, "No."

A new patio? I said, "No."

How about an outdoor deck? I said, "No."

Then he asked if he could interest me in a concrete pink flamingo for our yard. I laughed. He hung up.

December 23. Doris, Pat, and I were invited by Doris' granddaughter, LaRae, to help her and her fourth grade classmates pull taffy at the Phelps Hotel. We were told they wanted someone who knew how to do it, and none of us wanted to admit how many years had passed since our last taffy pull, so we accepted the challenge. It was a fun afternoon and brought back fond memories. The children decorated a Christmas tree with folded paper dove ornaments, popcorn garlands, and candles they made during the afternoon. They also decorated gingerbread people and gingerbread trees. This was an old-fashioned Christmas that we enjoyed as much as the fourth graders did.

A side note — we were to wear pioneer clothing, which I didn't know until two hours before we were supposed to be there. I was frantic and finally ended up wearing my best printed long flannel nightgown, with a sash made out of a roll of blanket binding. Pat loaned me a white crocheted shawl to complete my ensemble, and I was ready to go. This was really make-do, but the pioneers had to make do with whatever was on hand at the time, so I guess I really got into the spirit of the day.

December 24. One thing I know the family will miss this year is me playing "White Christmas" on the piano while Robin sings. This is a ritual she and I used to practice every year. Practice is the correct word. Robin has a beautiful voice, but I know it was difficult for her to sing to my piano accompaniment. "White Christmas" is the only song I ever knew how to play all the way through on the piano, and what should've been a five minute performance, took me about thirty minutes to get through. It was sort of like playing a record on the slowest speed possible. By the time we finished, we usually discovered we were the only ones left in the room.

December 25. Christmas is here, and our house is filled with joy. Robin, her fiancé Ron, Michael, Jillian, Shelly the turtle, and Simon the cat, have come to spend the holidays with us.

For the first time in my life, I had tears in my eyes when I unwrapped one of my presents. Robin gave me a stuffed doll with granny features, wearing a purple dress, a feathered hat, and red shoes with baggy hose. To go with the doll, Robin had my favorite poem printed and framed. It really touched my heart. The poem is "When I Am An Old Woman" by Jenny Joseph.

Bob's mother, Nellie, and his sister, Jean, joined us for the Christmas dinner. After we ate, we played our traditional bingo game, which is Nellie's favorite thing to do. I always wrap all the things I couldn't get rid of throughout the year for the bingo prizes, and have a rule that they have to keep what they win.

I have to mention one thing about cooking the Christmas dinner. Ron is an excellent cook, and I wonder if I had him fooled when he walked into the kitchen to see me standing at the sink mashing a sauce through a strainer with a spoon. I'm hoping he assumed it was a gourmet way of cooking in western Nebraska. What I was really doing was trying to mash the lumps out of the gravy.

December 26. I awoke in the middle of the night and wondered if it was yesterday or today. I finally got up to see. The clock said 11:45 P.M., so it was still yesterday. Then I thought, "No, that's impossible. Whatever day it is now, it's always today."

So, I guess, it can never be yesterday while it's today. I'm glad I don't have to worry about if it's today or tomorrow, or is that the same thing? I think I'll just go back to bed until today gets here.

December 27. The second Christmas shift has arrived. Kevin, Mary, Brandon, Sam and Katie have come, so happily, we get to enjoy Christmas Day again. Wouldn't it be great to have twelve children and have holiday visits occur every month. Then, we'd have Christmas all year long.

December 28. One of our gifts wasn't a big hit with the recipient. We gave Sam a rock tumbler that was on his "really want wish list." Who was to know the rocks had to tumble for 48 hours without looking at them, then change the solution and tumble them for eight more days before they were finished? We also discovered this should be done in a closet, as quietness is not one of the features of a rock tumbler.

It was definitely not an "enjoy now" toy. Oh, well, maybe we'll be more of a hit next year.

December 29. The Christmas decorations were put away today for another year. Why is it so enjoyable to put them up, and such a relief to take them down? I guess that's where the saying "You can have too much of a good thing" comes from.

I still have 149 candy canes left. I think I'll crush them, bag them, and sell them as toppings for ice cream, puddings, and cakes.

December 30. Why do magazine companies send out several subscription renewal notices? Each time we get one, we can't remember if we renewed or not, so we have to go back in our file several months to check for sure. If we don't find any verification that we've already renewed, we're still not sure, as it might be in the mail, so we just stick the notice in another file and immediately forget about it until we get another notice. Then we start the process all over again. It gets to be such a hassle. Maybe we should just let all our subscriptions lapse to simplify our lives.

December 31. Michael is seventeen today. He was born in Julesburg, Colorado, where the town showers the first baby of the new year with gifts. He missed that by forty-five minutes.

Michael is the most kind, gentle, caring young adult I know. Except when it comes to playing chess with his grandmother. Then, he becomes downright bloodthirsty.

January

January 1. Happy New Year. I have my resolution list made, and probably for the first time in my life, I know I'll keep my resolutions this year. Here is my list.
   1. I won't worry about dieting.
   That's my list, and yes, I know this is the same resolution I made last fall, but if something works well, I stick with it.

January 2. Robin and I have always been mistaken for each other on the telephone. Once when she was visiting us, her fiancé, Ron, called to talk to her and I answered the telephone. He hesitantly said, "Am I speaking to the most beautiful girl in the world?"
   I said, "Yes." We chatted a minute or two and I asked him if he would like to speak to the other most beautiful girl in the world.
   Ron answered, "I thought I was."
   I said, "Well, don't despair. Robin will get better with age."

January 3. The National Education Recognition Awards are to be given to outstanding educators soon. This year, they're adding a new award for an outstanding educator not in the teaching field. I expect to get notification that I've won that award any day now. After all, I've been trying to educate people to my way of thinking for years.

January 4. Home remedies are slowly becoming a thing of the past. One of my favorites was the tried and true method of removing a wart. Take a raw potato and cut it in half. Rub the raw portion over the wart. My childhood experience with this has taught me it really works, but not without the final magical step. When you have finished rubbing the wart with the potato, you must tie the halves together with string and bury them in the backyard.

January 5. Bob and I had a slight communication problem this morning. He was telling me he read in to-day's newspaper that an estimated 20,000,000 monarchs died in a snowstorm in Mexico.

I said, "How did they get that many rulers in one place?"

He sighed, "Monarch butterflies. A ruler is something you measure inches with."

January 6. Shortly after Bob left for town this afternoon, he received an important phone call. I told the caller I'd try to locate Bob and have him return the call.

How wonderful it is to live in a small town. I called the gas station, and asked their secretary, Joyce, if Bob was there. She said, "He was here this morning. I'll check to see if he came back." When she returned to the phone, she said, "No, he's not here now, but you can reach him at the elevator."

January 7. Katie is five years old today. She told me her favorite thing at our house to see is Sophie, our basset hound. She spends hours when she's here with Sophie, petting her, brushing her, and singing love songs to her.

I'm not sure where Grandpa and Grandma rank on her "happy to see" list, but I hope we place second and third, at least.

January 8. Bob and I don't train dogs for a living, which is a good thing. On the other side of the coin, our dogs have done quite well at training us. They've taught us to throw a ball for them. They've taught us that when they don't run after the ball, but sit in front of us, looking back and forth, from us to the ball, that we are supposed to fetch the ball for them. They've taught us that one bark means open the door. They've taught us that sitting by their dish and looking in our direction means "Feed Me."

Somewhere down the line, we've failed to communicate to the dogs that we're the masters.

January 9. Farm specialists have just informed the farmers that if you have more than 700 grasshoppers in a field, there is a problem.

A picture forms in my mind. The farmers are in their fields counting, one, two, three, four, five, six, seven, eight, and half way through the counting, one of the grasshoppers gets out of line, and they have to start the counting all over again.

Farm specialists don't come from real farms, do they?

January 10. Let's go back to the days when you dialed a telephone number and actually got to talk to a real live person. I ordered a badly needed winter coat today, as my old one is into it's 25th year of wear. I dialed the telephone number provided in the catalog, and got a voice that told me this was a voice-activated service, which meant that whatever I said went automatically on my order. I got so confused, that I won't know until my order comes, whether I ordered the coat number or the credit card number in gold.

This voice told me before I hung up if there were any more questions pertaining to my order, they'd be contacting me by telephone. That means I'm compelled to sit here by the phone until it rings, as I have no doubt that they'll have questions for me. I just hope when they call back that it isn't voice-activated. My patience is wearing thin, and it's so frustrating to argue with a machine.

January 11. Bob and I are in love. No, not with each other—well yes that, too—but we finally traded our fifteen-year-old car in for a new baby blue. Well, not new—used—but new to us. It's amazing. The doors open, it starts when you turn on the ignition, hums instead of wheezes, and the heater actually heats.

Someone asked me if we didn't feel an attachment with our old car that served us faithfully for so many years. I said, "No. It's difficult to form a bond with a piece of machinery, that can't be broken if something better comes along."

January 12. I'm going to bake a poppy seed cake. The recipe called for a can of poppy seed filling. Most of the grocery store clerks didn't have a clue as to what it was. They usually tried to sell me poppy seed in one ounce jars, which meant I would've had to buy thirteen jars of them at a cost of $16.77. I finally located a 12 ounce can of poppy seed filling at a cost of $3.39.

My first reaction was that it was too expensive, anyway. I did buy it, after I thought about how difficult it must have been to open all those tiny, tiny seeds to fill a 12-ounce can with poppy seed filling.

January 13. It has been proven, and I can attest to it, that arthritis settles in bones that have been broken. I have broken my right arm twice, my left arm three times, my right leg in three places, my left shoulder once, the little finger on my right hand once, and four of my ribs have been cracked. Arthritis has found its way to all those parts. What concerns me is the part I'm guessing to be the next fall to the clutches of arthritis. That part is my twice broken nose.

January 14. The winter doldrums were starting to get to some of us, so this evening, Margaret, Doris, Bob and I gathered at Pat and Willie's for a pot luck soup supper and a few games of six-handed 13 point pitch. Bob and I hadn't played pitch for 15 years, so part of the time was spent teaching us how. We all enjoyed the evening so much, we decided to repeat it at least once a month.

It made me wonder what else Bob and I enjoyed 15 years ago that we could do now, that wouldn't require a lot of physical effort.

January 15. One chore I never plan on doing again is one I deftly avoided in my youth. When I married Bob, my mother-in-law, Nellie, informed me I must learn this task if I intended to be a farmer's wife. I learned it well and hated it. It was cleaning chickens. To this day, I can still visualize a headless chicken flopping around on the ground, and smell the scent of singed feathers.

That is why I always sit a naked chicken upright on the kitchen counter and have a long, heart to heart talk with it before I put it in the roaster for Sunday dinner. Atonement is good for the soul.

January 16. Speaking of chickens, while Bob and I lived on the farm, I knew for a fact that chickens were not the gentle innocent creatures everyone believed them to be.

Gathering eggs was one of my chores, which I looked forward to in fear. I always wore gloves, and like Teddy Roosevelt, spoke softly and carried a big stick, for the daily ritual. After taking a deep breath, I cautiously opened the chicken coop door to see the chickens sitting on their nests in battle formation. I'd very carefully raise the hens with the stick, work my way along the length of the stick, and reach under them with my gloved hand to lift the eggs from the nest. Once the eggs were all gathered, I backed out of the chicken coop door, so as not to be attacked from the rear.

Looking back, I guess I was making more out of it than was necessary. Although, I can still see the headlines that might have read, "Farm wife severely injured in pecking attack from pet chickens."

January 17. My mother made Bob and me a lovely standing anniversary book using our wedding picture. She gave it to us on our 25th wedding anniversary.

I was looking at it today, and surprisingly, didn't feel a loss of my youth. I was simply comforted to notice the picture is wrinkling with age, just as Bob and I are.

January 18. I enjoy playing those hand-held computer games. My favorite is the poker game. I like that fact that you can take these games with you and play them anywhere. Bob even asked me if I would like to have it sewn permanently to my hip, so I could always have it close at hand.

That's silly, but I've started sewing pockets on all my clothes to accommodate the game.

January 19. Our daughter was married today. Robin married Ron Peterson, a genuinely great guy, in a simple home wedding ceremony in Red Cloud, Nebraska. Robin looked beautiful in an ivory lace dress over a teal sheath and Ron was princely in an ivory tuxedo. Michael, handsome in black and white with a teal tie, gave his mother in marriage and Jillian, lovely in off-white, was her mother's maid-of-honor.

I, as mother-of-the-bride, cried traditionally, because I was happy for them—yes. But, also because I had to imagine the whole ceremony. Oh, the wedding really happened, but Bob and I couldn't get there because the highway was closed for 180 miles of the trip to all traffic, as were all other roads, due to heavy ice conditions.

We were with them in spirit and wish them all love and happiness.

January 20. What great friends I have. Yesterday, Doris, Pat, and Margaret just happened to drop in with a bag of homemade chocolate cookies. I made coffee and we just sat around and visited. Not a word was said about why they came, but I knew it was to cheer me because I couldn't get to Robin's wedding.

Good friends are like expensive chocolates you savor and enjoy, and never tire of.

January 21. Bob likes his hot dogs stuffed with cheese, wrapped in bacon and broiled. I don't broil them often, because it seems such a waste of time to clean the broiler for two small hot dogs.

I came up with a great idea. I poked holes in a large aluminum pie tin and placed it over a smaller aluminum pie tin to catch the drips. It worked superbly, and when the hot dogs were done and placed on the table, I removed the upper pie tin to discover the bottom pie tin had pre-punched holes in it, too. The drips had found their way to the bottom of the oven. Now, I have to clean the whole oven, when cleaning the broiler pan may have been easier after all.

January 22. Speaking of cooking, our smoke detector goes off a lot when I'm cooking. As Bob runs to see what's happening, I plod through the smoke to tell him, "Relax. I'm just testing the smoke detector."

January 23. One of my best friends is such a classy lady. She's always so together, that the day she accidentally wore a pair of unmatched earrings to church astonished me.

Bob suggested I give her a pair of mismatched earring as a gift. I have one odd earring in my jewelry box, so as soon as I lose an earring from another pair, I'll be able to give her a gift designed for her alone.

January 24. Isn't it difficult to break old habits? When Kevin and Mary gave Bob and me a portable phone, I spent weeks standing by the phone base with the portable at my ear, while stretching as far as I could to reach my cup of coffee with my free hand. I was so sure if I moved too much, the connection would be broken immediately.

January 25. When I laid eyes on the first bubble hair cut, I had no idea what I was seeing. Jillian was sporting the do and stayed to visit while Robin ran some errands.

Jillian said, "Grandma, my hair is cut a little uneven in the back. Will you straighten it for me?"

I got my scissors out, thinking I could quickly repair the damage. Happily, I clipped away, evened the back up nicely, and unknowingly, destroyed the "bubble" completely. I felt awful when I was told what I'd done, but Jillian was a trooper and bit back tears, as she told me, "That's okay, Grandma. It'll grow back."

I have to admit, that to this day when I see a bubble hair-do, I have to fight the temptation to run for my scissors.

January 26. They say that gingko improves your memory, so I bought some gingko tablets for Bob and me. I reached for the bottle this morning and stopped with my hand in midair, because I couldn't remember if I'd already taken a tablet or not. Evidently, it requires more than one tablet for them to have an effect.

January 27. Do you know a lot about antiques? I don't but I do know about antiques of the heart. I have an old treadle sewing machine that belonged to my grandmother that I can't part with. I learned to sew on it. I have an old lawyer's bookshelf that belonged to my step-grandfather that came with a complete set of Kipling's works, to which we've added our own small library. I also have a little wooden rocker that hold memories of my grandmother rocking her grandchildren, my mother rocking me, and me rocking my children and grandchildren.

These antiques aren't for sale. They're a part of me.

January 28. I need to clean the bathroom shelves. One shelf is stacked full of partially used face cream jars. There has to be enough dabs of cream left in them to grease all the squeaky hinges in town.

There is a reason that I have so many jars of beauty cream. I'm sure I'm only one jar away from finding that one jar of wrinkle cream that will miraculously change me overnight into a Miss America contender. Maybe the magic is in the next jar that I have yet to uncap.

January 29. Jean visited the other night with a jigsaw puzzle tucked under her arm, which she and I put together in three hours. Well, it gave me jigsaw fever, so I decided to start another puzzle today to while away the dreary winter days.

In our home, the best place to put a jigsaw puzzle together is at our eating table, and as I neglected to check out the dimensions of the puzzle, the table is now covered with 1500 puzzle pieces, that when completed will measure three feet by two feet. This might take a day or two, but in the meantime, I'm sure Bob won't mind eating off the floor.

January 30. Pat entrusted me with babysitting her lovely houseplants while she and Willie are visiting their son, Matt, and his bride in Arizona for a few weeks.

Well, wouldn't you know, the largest of her plants was hanging limply over the sink the first day I went to water them. I've gone every day since, to see how it's doing, and so far, there's no improvement. Short of mouth to mouth resuscitation, I don't know what else to do, except pray.

January 31. Fred, that's the name I've given to the wilting plant at Pat's, doesn't look any better today. I'm beginning to panic. Even if I could locate a plant exactly like Fred, I couldn't replace him today, as it's fifteen degrees below zero outside. I'll keep praying.

February 1. I have proof positive that prayer works. Fred is recovering. I checked on him again this morning, and I'm sure as I turned around to leave, I felt him give me a pat on the back with one of his huge leaves.

February 2. Groundhog Day. I know if the groundhog sees his shadow, we're to have six more weeks of winter. How dependable can that forecast be, if the groundhog's dumb enough to go outside without earmuffs and a scarf, when the temperature is already twenty degrees below zero?

February 3. Bob has decided when he retires in two years as Big Springs Precinct Deuel County Commissioner, he is going to run for the Big Springs Airport Authority Board.

This will be a sure thing, as Big Springs has no Airport Authority Board. For that matter, Big Springs has no airport. I think, just maybe, he's due for retirement.

February 4. Margaret called to ask if we were getting four of the cable stations on our television set that she couldn't get on hers. I checked and we were getting them. To make matters worse, some of the buttons on her TV remote control weren't working either. These modern conveniences have spoiled all of us.

It reminded me of the time many years ago when Margaret and Melvin, and Bob and I had the first TV sets in the country and only one station to watch. We would call each other excitedly on our party-line if we got snow on our sets. One day, Margaret had to call the repairmen, because their television wouldn't come in at all. He came out and plugged it in for her.

February 5. How am I ever going to lose weight? We neighbor ladies are deeply into spontaneous "drop everything" coffees. The other day, Doris brought yummy cinnamon rolls, and she and Margaret came for coffee. Two days later, Doris, Elaine, and I went to Margaret's for yummy date cookies and coffee. I guess I'll introduce yummy celery sticks to our coffees, but I doubt that will be a big hit.

February 6. Today is Pat's birthday. Pat's enthusiasm and zest for life are a joy to behold. She's a mother of six grown children and grandmother of twenty-one. She looks ten years younger than she really is. She makes beautiful quilts, sews, crochets, knits, paints ceramics and actually enjoys cooking, to name a few of her activities.

One day last November, I visited her in the early afternoon and she was making Christmas wreaths and baking cookies. But that was not enough, she'd already raked their yard of leaves and repaired an eight foot long crack in their kitchen wall.

As Pat is vacationing in Arizona, Doris, Margaret and I felt compelled to somehow acknowledge her birthday, so we spent the day shopping in North Platte, Nebraska.

February 7. Robin and I call each other on the telephone on alternate week-ends and sometimes, in between. I've figured a solution to bring our telephone bills back down to mole hills instead of the mountains they are now.

The next time Robin, Ron, Michael, and Jillian come to visit, I'm going to give them a very large ball of twine when they leave. I will tie one end to our bedpost and they can string it out behind them on their 250 mile journey to their home. They can then tie an empty soup can to their end of the twine, and I'll do the same on our end. And there we'll have it, free instant communication.

February 8. Margaret's birthday is today. She and I have been friends for over 43 years. We were neighbors first on the farm, and we now live only one block apart in town, and still remain friends. That's an enduring friendship.

February 9. I made a pumpkin pie this morning that turned into a very costly project. In the middle of making the filling, I ran out of cloves. The empty jar of spice must be very old because the sticker price on it is $1.29. A quick trip to the grocery store for a new jar of cloves put me into instant shock. The fresh jar has a price tag of $5.77 for the same amount of spice as was in the old jar.

There is one small consolation. This jar of cloves, handled with tender, loving care, should last for the next twenty years.

February 10. I don't believe this. The radio's national news reported this morning that the surgeon general is going to put warning labels on sporting goods products warning "couch potatoes" that "lack of exercise is detrimental to your health." Excuse me? How many of us "couch potatoes" are going to go out and purchase sporting goods?

February 11. Don't you get aggravated with the lottery sweepstakes winners who act so surprised and gush, "I never dreamed I'd win. I've never won anything before in my life."

When I win I'll only have three words to say. "It's about time."

February 12. I went with Pat and Doris to Ogallala today. When we got home, Bob came out to the car to help me carry seven huge shopping bags into the house.

As Bob's eyes and mouth gaped open, I said, "You're lucky honey. I just went along for the ride."

February 13. Something I think the kids these days are missing out on is the enjoyment of an old-fashioned small town Saturday night. The whole family piled in the car and went downtown early to find a choice parking spot on main street where all the activities could be viewed. Mom and dad did their week's shopping, as the stores always stayed open until 9:00 at night. The younger kids got their allowance and were treated to a trip to the dime store, where hours could be spent deciding which of the five-for-a-penny candy to buy. The young lovers strolled hand in hand on their way to a movie or the band concert in the park. Friends and neighbors visited at each others' cars, and sometimes the whole family went to the Saturday night public dance to round out the evening.

February 14. Valentine's Day. Jillian decided there was a possibility that she wouldn't be receiving any gifts on this day, so she sent herself flowers. I like her way of thinking.

February 15. Sophie is a dog that's full of love for one and all. One day, when Robin, Michael, Jillian, and Shelly, their pet turtle, were visiting, we couldn't find Shelly anywhere when they were ready to leave. Locating a lost turtle isn't as easy as you may think. They don't come when you whistle, or call their name, and make absolutely no sound to track them with.

Unbeknownst to us, Sophie had picked up Shelly in her mouth and went outside for play time. She was happily running around the backyard with Shelly held gently in her mouth. Sophie was grinning from ear to ear, and when Shelly was rescued, she was too. Or maybe it was a grimace, as her shell still carries the scar where one of Sophie's teeth carried her a little too lovingly.

February 16. Our newer-used car has people looking at me strangely and shaking their heads. It may be because I find myself talking to it. These new-fangled gadgets confuse me.

The lights go on automatically when I start the car and I say, "Please, don't do that. It's still daylight outside."

The little picture of the man keeps flashing red and dings at me if I haven't got my seat belt fastened, and I say, "Give me time. I'm doing it as fast as I can."

If I run back in the house to get something I've forgotten, I leave the keys in the ignition, and the whole car starts dinging at me. I say, "Relax. I'll be back in a minute."

It was easier with our old car. If I goofed up, I always knew everyone would blame the car because it was so old. Now, I suspect they blame me, but I can use my age as an excuse.

February 17. Our bathroom sink has been dripping maddeningly for several weeks. Steve and Charlene, owners of the Big Springs Country Supply Store, have been kind enough to order the cartridges that are needed to stop the annoying drip. The supply company keeps sending them cabinet latches instead. Maybe it would be best to just build a cabinet, using latches, around the sink. Then, we couldn't see or hear the drip.

February 18. One doesn't always inherit the talents of their parents. My mother taught baking to 4-H children and specialized in breads.

When it's my turn to furnish bread for our neighborhood card suppers, I head straight for the grocery store and pick up a package of refrigerated biscuits. Like bad yeast, I don't always rise to the occasion.

February 19. Today is President's Day. Happy birthday to all of you. My favorite President was Harry S. Truman. I have to admit, I didn't realize how good he was until he was no longer our President. He had an earthy, down-home attitude that is missing in later politicians. He took the flack himself with his "The Buck Stops Here" theory. I've found that the Presidents who follow him try very hard to find someone else to blame their problems on.

February 20. When Robin, Ron, Michael, and Jillian are visiting, we naturally have extra laundry. One day, during their last visit, I was drying a load of clothes in the dryer. Our washer and dryer are in the kitchen area and the noise sometimes goes over the top of the decibel scale.

Robin took a load out of the dryer to put away, and looking at Ron's bib overalls quizzically, said, "What's this?"

I replied, "Ingenuity." I'd pinned a hand towel around the buckles on the bib to muffle the sound.

Robin just shook her head and said, "Of course."

February 21. I finally got my badly needed new glasses today. There's a whole new world out there. Our senses of sight, hearing, smell, touch, and taste are taken for granted a lot of the time. Anyway, my sense of smell isn't good, but when I say, "I don't smell good," all I get from people are affirmative nods. Now, what does that mean?

February 22. Harold and June visited Bob and me this evening. We went to the Char-Bar for their Thursday night special, which is delicious chicken-fried steak. As we were entering the restaurant, we met Ed and Loree, our gardening neighbors, who were just leaving. They had gone out for supper to celebrate their 60th wedding anniversary. Loree told me she didn't want to celebrate before the day actually arrived, just in case they got divorced before then.

February 23. As I grow older, I've discovered I'm shorter than I once was. Therefore, I have more skin left over than I need to cover my body. This extra skin hanging from my upper arms and neck must be there for a purpose. I guess the surplus neck skin could be wrapped around and used as a scarf in winter for warmth. I haven't quite figured out what to do with my flabby arms yet. Maybe I'll starch them and pretend I'm sprouting angel wings.

February 24. Farmers must have their income tax returns in by the first of March. There's a shortage of farmers. There's also a shortage of prisons, and I'm wondering if all the farmers refused to pay their taxes what would they do with us. Would they change the tax laws, or would they just tax us more in order to build more prisons to put us in?

February 25. It's our turn to have the neighbors for a soup supper and card evening. I've decided to make chicken and dumplings. My dumpling recipe calls for butter the size of an egg. This is my Grandma Ida's recipe, which may explain the directions.

Grandma Ida always gave her recipes willingly to anyone who asked for one. No one knew until many years later that she gave the correct recipes selectively. If she liked you on the day you asked for a recipe, you got the correct one. If she was upset with you on that day, you got a recipe that was just wrong enough that yours never tasted quite as good as hers.

She was my favorite grandperson, and I've got the correct custard pie recipe.

February 26. Something has occurred to me. When I took care of Pat's flowers while she and Willie were on vacation, several of the plants almost died. When I took care of Jillian's fish aquarium over one summer vacation, several of the fish died.

Pat's flowers died because I overwatered them. Can you overwater fish too?

February 27. Bob suggested that if I titled this book *The Private Sex Life of a 65-Year-Old Housewife*, that I might actually sell a few copies before people found out what it's really about.

February 28. I have a backache and discovered when I got the pills out of the medicine chest for lower back pain, the instructions on the bottle were in such fine print, I had to hunt for the magnifying glass to see what the dosage was. Don't the pharmaceutical companies realize that when a person gets old enough to have all these aches and pains, that their eyesight is probably slipping too? They make large print on playing cards. It seems like they should be able to do the same on a pill bottle.

February 29. Leap year has leaped today. Years ago, this was the one day in the year that girls could ask boys for a date. Now, this is an accepted daily occurrence, so I wonder what the girls do to make this a special day in today's world.

Regardless, I now have an extra day that wasn't on my schedule. I guess I'll just have to adjust.

March 1. March didn't come in like a lion or a lamb. It came in more like a rabbit aspiring to be a kangaroo with a lot of bravado on kind of a wimpy day.

March 2. I believe in the protection of animals and I don't wear anything with fur on it, but I heard something today that disturbed me. The people who create costumes for Barbie have been forced to remove any fur pieces used on her attire.

How do the people who are protesting know that the fur used on Barbie's clothes isn't a public service in disguise? They could've merely been using fur from highway road kill.

March 3. I'm finally getting used to my new eyeglasses with trifocals. I guess I feel confident enough now to confess what happened to me on the day I first put them on.

When I left the optometrist's office with my brand-new glasses on, I walked to our car in the parking lot. Sitting in the car next to ours was a gentleman who nodded and smiled at me. I smiled back, got into our car, and prepared to exit the parking lot. I backed up and proceeded forward to drive straight ahead, right off the curb. I glanced in the rearview mirror and the nice gentleman was looking my way, holding his head in his hands and shaking it back and forth. Since the optometrist's office also houses a dentist, I could only assume the poor man was suffering from an excruciating toothache.

March 4. I'm still waiting for the body fairy to tap me with her magic wand while I sleep and restore my girlish figure overnight. I'm beginning to think that's as futile as waiting for the tooth fairy to grant me a third set of teeth.

March 5. Where's the background music in real life that always warns you of impending danger in the movies? I could've used it when I tripped over the throw rug in the kitchen, fell down, and skidded to an abrupt halt at the refrigerator. The only music I heard were the groaning sounds I made, after the fact.

March 6. I wonder if our pets view us as their pets? I wonder if they think of us as unfortunate beings who must walk on their hind legs and wear clothing to cover our furless bodies? I wonder if they think our main purpose on earth is to serve their needs? I wonder, sometimes, if they're right?

March 7. Reading is one of my favorite things to do. Our town library is a source of joy to me. Besides being one of the best stocked libraries in the area I can always look forward to a visit with Mary Beth, the librarian and Judy her assistant.

Mary Beth and our daughter Robin are good friends. Judy and our daughter-in-law Mary are also good friends. This creates a warm atmosphere for our chats while I browse for a good mystery to take home to read.

March 8. I just won $100 on a Nebraska scratch lottery ticket. So I decided now would be a good time to replace our chipped and cracked everyday dishes. I also decided to add to our shortage of flatware. Our pillows are in bad shape and they are on sale today, so I decided now would also be a good time to replace them. So far I've spent $150 of the $100 I won.

March 9. George Burns died today at the age of 100. I felt as if I'd lost a family member or a dear friend. Bob and I grew up with George's wit and humor. He may be gone, but his wit and humor will live forever.

March 10. Bob and I actually traveled over the weekend. We went to Red Cloud to visit Robin, Ron, Michael, and Jillian. Kevin, Mary, Brandon, Sam, and Katie were there for a visit also. It was a rare treat for us since we are seldom able to have our family together in the same place at the same time.

Ron is a fantastic cook. He grilled thick marinated steaks, accompanied by cheese and garlic mashed potatoes, garlic French bread, and buttered corn. Norma June, Ron's mother, furnished a yummy chocolate cake for dessert. We overate and thoroughly enjoyed doing it.

After our meal, we were treated to a home movie of Ron and Robin's wedding. We felt like we were actually able to attend the nuptials after all. When the movie was over, Michael and Jillian performed the skit they were scheduled to do for the school speech contest. Michael played his saxophone for us. His repertoire included "Yakkity Sax" which is one of Bob's favorites. Not that we're prejudiced, but our grandchildren are very talented.

We had a wonderful visit, but I still fail to comprehend why our children and their families chose to live so far from civilization.

March 11. We humans are creatures of comfort. Our neighbors are putting their electric lines underground. The electric company man asked me if it would be all right if they shut the electricity off for an hour and a half.

Not even flinching, I said, "Sure."

I wanted a cup of coffee, so I hurried to make a pot before the electricity went off. Thinking I was clever, I discovered the coffee soon cooled. Thinking ahead again, I tried to warm it in the microwave oven. Wrong.

Then I thought, "I'll vacuum." Wrong.

How about ironing? Wrong

Guess I'll just relax and watch some television. Wrong.

Ah ha. I finally thought of something I can do that isn't wired. Read a book. I can enjoy that until it gets dark anyway, since the hour and a half has already been three and a half hours.

March 12. I feel obligated to have a dinner and invite all those people who have helped me with my cooking through the years. The guest list would include Mrs. Smith, Sara Lee, Colonel Sanders, Master Doughboy, Mr. and Mrs. Swanson, Mr. and Mrs. Lipton, Mr. and Mrs. Stouffer, Mr. and Mrs. Campbell, Betty Crocker and Duncan Hines.

Our table only seats eight comfortably and I'm sure I would forget someone that should be on the list. I think I'll just send thank you notes instead.

March 13. I've just blown another myth to shreds. I grew up believing a high forehead signified intelligence. Having a high forehead, I assumed this put me right up there with the geniuses of the world. That isn't true. I now realize that I just have a receding hairline. The fact that it took me some sixty-odd years to figure that out proves the myth to be a fairy tale.

March 14. Our clothes date from the jitterbug era to a period somewhere in the early 1990s. So where does all the lint come from when these clothes are laundered and dried in the dryer? I figured lint was what was holding our clothing together. I'm sure on the day when there's no lint in the trap, I'll open the dryer to find our clothes have disintegrated completely.

March 15. Today is Charlie and Twyla's 43rd wedding anniversary. We helped them celebrate their 25th anniversary and three years ago we were there for their 40th anniversary.

Their daughter Charlene and Robin are the same age and were school chums. Also their son Terry and Kevin were buddies. Memories of our common ties go back many years.

March 16. I've enrolled in a computer class. I find it hard to believe. I'll be the oldest student in the class but I'm going to give it a try. Mostly I want to see the look of surprise on my grandchildren's faces when I drop a word or two of computer lingo into our chats. I can almost hear them begging, "Delete Grandma, delete."

March 17. St. Patrick's Day. Bob is half-Irish and has a tendency to lapse into an Irish brogue if Ireland is mentioned. This will be the language today until he sleeps it off overnight. This will be one long day of feeling I've been transported to the land of the "wee people."

March 18. I'm proud of the fact that Robin and Kevin are neat people. They're neat as in "great" and also neat as in "tidy." Kevin was so neat when he was still living at home that he'd always arrange his clothes for the next day's wear the night before. Shirt, underwear, trousers, socks, and shoes were all lined up neatly in a row — on the floor.

March 19. Don't you hate it when the phone rings and whoever is calling hangs up just as you pick it up? That happened to me today and four hours later I still don't know who called. I called the Publisher's Clearing House right away to see if they tried to reach me. It wasn't them. I guess it couldn't have been very important.

March 20. Today is the first day of spring. For some reason, it doesn't seem any different than the last day of winter. There should be something more definitive about spring than the fact that white shoes are now acceptable to wear.

March 21. I have uncovered the fallacy of another myth. It isn't true that you lose the hair on your head as you grow older. What's really happening is that it just grows inward and comes out your nose and ears instead.

March 22. We've had terrible weather the last few days. This didn't deter me when that call came for coffee and fresh cinnamon rolls at Doris's. Of course, this called for major planning. I got the car out, drove half a block to pick up Pat, drove another half block to pick up Margaret, and another half block to arrive at Doris's. The rolls and coffee were worth the journey.

Like the postal service, we don't let rain, sleet, nor snow deter us from our appointed rounds.

March 23. I was sorting through our pile of unanswered mail today and ran across an old offer to obtain a genealogy chart for the Robb family. I asked Bob if he still wanted to order it. He said, "No, that's been lying around for several months. They've probably chopped down our family tree by now."

March 24. Yesterday was Ardis' birthday and today is Edith's birthday. Edith and Ardis are good friends from Oshkosh, Nebraska. Bob and I met them shortly after we met Harold and June. About twelve years ago, in our dancing days, they helped keep Bob's dancing feet from gathering moss.

March 25. I sent for a free booklet on wills and estates. This is a joke in itself in our case. A form and instructions for making out your own will was inside. The form was to be filled in with Bob's name and age followed by the word "Spouse" and a blank space. I asked Bob if I should write "yes" in the blank space. He said, "No. Just put one."

March 26. My step-grandfather always insisted on a properly set table at mealtime. The correct silver was aligned in order with the butter knife placed horizontally on a separate bread plate. Dressings and sauces were served in a small stoppered cruet and butter was molded into designed pats and placed over ice in a butter bowl.

I inherited the butter bowl and the stoppered cruet but in our home they're merely conversation pieces.

March 27. I've been pondering the fact that my new trifocal eyeglasses cost $288 and that's just for the lenses and examination. I kept my old frames.

I remember as a young child going with my Grandma Ida when she purchased her new glasses. She did this every two years. It involved a trip to the dime store where Grandma stood at the counter trying on several pairs of glasses and reading the hand-held chart that was provided. When she decided on a pair that suited her, she paid the clerk the $1.50 and we were off. This procedure is beginning to make a lot of sense to me now.

March 28. The Agriculture Women's luncheon was held in Ogallala. Margaret invited Pat, Doris, and me to go with her. Free lunch? Sure! We went. There was a nice crowd and speaker. We had good food and had a great time.

It was early afternoon when we arrived back in Big Springs, but too late to start on a work project and too early to go home. We decided to gather at Margaret's home so Pat could teach us a new card game called "Nil." I'm getting better at learning how to lose graciously. To be honest, I still prefer winning and gloating.

March 29. Margaret said she accidentally sprayed her armpits with lemon furniture polish instead of deodorant. I laughed.

Elaine said her cousin had rubbed a hair depilatory on his already thinning hair instead of hair cream. I laughed.

Doris said she sprayed her arthritic knee with WD40 oil. I laughed. I laughed one time too often. She was serious because when you think about it, arthritic joints are really nothing more than rusty hinges.

March 30. You can't cry over spilled milk. But is it okay to cry over spilled money? I have a gallon jar full of silver dollars I've been saving. As I started to count them, the jar slipped out of my hands and I spilled them all down the heating vent.

No, it isn't true, but I thought it might be fun to see how many furnace repairmen would call to fix the furnace if I spread the story around.

March 31. This past week a major comet with an unpronounceable name passed through our skies and was visible to the naked eye. This comet only passes our way every 20,000 years so Bob and I felt obligated to locate it.

The first night we watched in awe as we found it in our northern skies. It was a long streak of reddish gold that shone brightly. We sat gazing at it for an enchanted hour.

The next night it was still in full view. We were enjoying this marvelous sight a second time when the telephone rang. It was Doris and she said, "Look out your west window. The comet is there and it's huge."

We looked and I was in awe again until Bob told me that I was just looking at the planet Jupiter. So, I went back to watching the comet's beautiful golden streak in our northern skies.

Later that night Bob stepped outside with Killer and Sophie for their nightly run and he located the real comet in our northeastern sky. It was a big, hazy, luminous ball. I was disappointed and slightly let down. I'd enjoyed the reddish gold streak much more.

What was the reddish gold streak we had happily viewed for two nights? Well, we discovered that was our neighbor's television antenna reflecting from the street light.

April 1. April Fool's Day. This used to be one of my favorite days. I believe though that Robin and Kevin have created a false memory of one April Fool's Day.

They attended a one-room country school and carried their lunches in Barbie and GI Joe lunch boxes everyday. One April Fool's Day, I made them each a sandwich of dry bread with a piece of paper for the filling on which I had written an April Fool's greeting. I placed these sandwiches on top of their usual peanut butter and jelly sandwiches.

To this day they both insist there was no real sandwich in their lunch boxes that day. Who's fooling whom?

April 2. I started and ended my computer class. I thought I'd be the oldest student. I wasn't but I surely was the greenest.

I thought the computer expertise was something I wanted to learn. It isn't.

I thought the computer would open a whole new territory for me. It does. It's called a state of confusion.

The computer community will have to learn to survive without my help. I'm sticking to my lead pencil with the handy attached eraser.

April 3. The trains, the elevator fans, and the railroad crews are all functioning simultaneously today. The sound of the whoos, the toots, the hums, and the whistles are steadily corroding my sanity.

I guess I'll just have to learn to live with it. There's as good a chance of removing them from my life as there is of starting a nudist colony in Alaska.

April 4. The brief lapses of memory as we age are sometimes laughable. A close friend called and asked if she was supposed to be doing something with me today.

I said, "No, not that I can remember."

She said that someone had asked her to do something with them today, but she couldn't remember who had asked her or what it was she was supposed to do.

I laughed, but when I hung up the phone, I started worrying. I began to wonder if doing this something with somebody also involved me. I couldn't remember it either.

April 5. Robin, Michael, and Jillian came late last night to spend an early Easter with us. I spent the whole day in the kitchen preparing the foods I know they enjoy.

My lineage has been traced to German, Canadian Indian, and English. Robin insists that I also must have been a Jewish mother in one of my previous lives. She says I'm always insisting that everyone eat more. I'll accept this because I'm also sure that a bowl of chicken soup cures most ailments.

April 6. Trying to work a three day visit into one day was difficult, but we did it. We ate. Michael taught me a card game called "Kings in the Corner." Jillian dyed Easter eggs. We ate. We watched a movie. We ate. I taught Robin, Michael, and Jillian how to play "Nil." We ate. We watched another movie. We ate. Robin and Jillian went looking for and found a prom dress for Jillian. Michael and I played "Scrabble." We ate. We watched yet another movie. We ate. It was a good day filled with love and heartburn.

April 7. Today is Easter. Has anyone ever figured out the connection between the Easter bunny and Easter eggs? This is not fair to the chickens. I don't know how the rabbit got this honor, but the chickens should holler "Fowl play." I know, that was a bad pun, but it really should be Easter chicken's day.

April 8. I watched our neighbors Jeannie and Layton fly a bird-shaped kite with their daughter and two sons. The view from our dining room window was peaceful and heart-warming. Sometimes, the simplest pleasures give the most joy to life.

April 9. Bob should've tied me to the bedpost this morning before he left for the day. I decided to repaint the bathroom. It didn't need repainting but I didn't care for the color I'd painted it last year. I thought, "I'll just mix up a color I like from all the leftover paint and it won't cost a thing except my time."

All went well until I started to replace the fixtures. The last thing to replace was the large bathroom mirror. I hung it in place without dropping it, but as I screwed in the last screw I heard something. Magically before my eyes appeared an eight inch crack.

So much for being thrifty. A new mirror is going to cost more than a gallon of paint ten times over. On top of all that I still don't care for the color but since I'm thoroughly disgusted, I'm going to ignore it.

April 10. How about the commercial on television about the couple who awaken in the morning and turn to each other for a morning kiss? She turns away saying "Not yet." She then jumps out of bed, runs to the bathroom, gargles, runs back to her mate and says, "Now I'm ready for that kiss."

Doesn't anyone notice that he didn't gargle?

April 11. I love this. I just love it. This has made my day. Scientists have discovered that the male brain starts shrinking when a male reaches the age of eighteen. The male reasoning power and memory start to fade at that age until at an elderly age they truly become grumpy old men. We females always wondered what the male problem was and now we have scientific proof. I just love it.

I'm sorry. Am I gloating?

April 12. I'm watching a spring and summer fashion show on television and I can see I am not going to be fashionable this summer. The rage is low-riding, long-legged tight pants with the belly button showing.

To wear these fashions, you'd have to be between the ages of ten and thirty, five-foot eight-inches tall, weigh no more than 105 pounds, and be shaped like a pencil. How many of us are built like that? I'm in my middle sixties, five-foot three inches tall, weigh 120 pounds and am shaped like a pear. Now just picture that. Boggles the mind doesn't it?

This had made me realize, if I were taller I'd be thinner.

April 13. When Bob buys a new pair of trousers, I automatically get out the scissors, needle, and thread. He insists he is as tall as he was twenty years ago. No way, but neither the tape measure nor the mirror have been able to convince him otherwise.

April 14. Bob says I have an excuse for everything I do wrong. He is wrong. I don't have an excuse for everything I do wrong. I have a reason for everything I do wrong. There is a big difference.

April 15. Income tax deadline day. I'm comforted to know our tax dollars are being spent wisely. The government is funding worthy causes, such as studying fly-fishing on three continents, studying the sex life of the mosquito and studying the brewing of beer in Africa.

April 16. Do you remember when a movie notified you of its finish with the simple words "The End?" Now, the credits at a movie's end seem to last almost as long as the movie. Does anyone ever really read these? It seems to me, if the movie studios wanted to be sure everyone would read all this information, from who produced the movie to who changed the broken light bulbs on the set, they should run the credits at the beginning of the film. That way people would feel obligated to stay in their seats waiting for the movie to start.

April 17. I had an early dental appointment this morning to have a broken tooth repaired. The dentist mentioned that he wished he had X-ray eyes like Superman to save him a lot of time. Then he said, "Did you know that the human head has thirty holes in it?"

I said, "No, but I do know the male brain starts to shrink at the age of eighteen." Then he gave me a Novocain shot. I think I should've waited until he was done working on my tooth before I made that remark. Five hours later, my mouth is still numb.

I hope it gets back to normal soon at least in time for me to go to Doris's for a neighborhood birthday coffee. The coffee is for me and I don't want to give the impression that one more year on my age has left me drooling coffee down my chin or missing my mouth altogether with a bite of cake.

P.S. I'm home from the coffee and my dentist will be happy to know I left no sweet unturned. Pat and Doris made the goodies and not wanting to offend either of them, I had some of everything, which included cinnamon rolls, sweet bread, macaroons, carrot cake and angel food cake. I have a feeling I'll be visiting my dentist again in the near future.

April 18. Well, it's here, no matter what I've done to try to avoid it. I'm another year older today. I refuse to say I'm over the hill and slowing down. I'm just gathering up speed to get to the top.

April 19. The solution to the economy slump is simple, which is probably why the politicians have never thought of it. Put every single product sold, from toenail clippers to private jet planes on sale with a 20 percent discount. All America, true to form, would run to the stores to buy everything in sight. Therein lies an instant economy cure.

April 20. I've always wanted a forsythia bush. I saw one in the store today and he begged to come home with me so I made his wish come true.

Now comes the hard part. If I can convince Bob that the spirea bush should be moved to a spot by the back door and the burning bush should be moved to where the spirea bush is now and the forsythia bush planted in the burning bush's present spot — I'll be happy.

Until I buy another bush.

April 21. I always knew our generation was smarter than those that have followed. Now I know why. A recent survey has shown that people who were given pacifiers as babies weren't as intelligent as those who weren't. Pacifiers weren't yet invented when our generation was in infancy, so we were already way ahead.

Although, do you know who is funding these surveys? We are. That's not such an intelligent move for our generation, is it?

April 22. Erma Bombeck died today at the age of sixty-nine. She was my idol. She taught us all how to laugh at ourselves. Her humor will be missed.

April 23. I had my laugh for the day at someone else's expense. I'm sorry about that, but I couldn't help it. I'll explain.

We'd been expecting the high pressure call that came today inquiring as to why we'd switched telephone companies. I told the very nice lady that called that we didn't care for their company's practice of laying off thousands of workers while the executives acquired huge bonuses for streamlining the company. She was obviously unaware of this. For the telephone conversation quickly turned to concern for her own job and the initial reason for which she called us was soon forgotten.

We had a real nice visit and were on a first name basis by the time our chat ended. We also made a promise to keep in touch.

April 24. When does a person stop being frugal and start becoming a pack rat? There's a fine line drawn between the two.

Am I frugal if I have a six-foot high tower of empty plastic containers that once held butter, whipped cream, or dips? Am I frugal if I have several stacks of women's magazines stored in the closet for future household references? Am I frugal if I have a gallon pail filled with empty pill bottles that just may come in handy for something someday? I think I've crossed the line.

April 25. We "Fabulous Four" ladies went shopping in North Platte the other day. When there are five of us, we are the "Fantastic Five Fillies." Six of us are the "Sexy Six." Seven of us are the "Sensational Seven." Eight of us are the — what was that? A yawn? Okay, I get the hint and I'll stop there. Besides, I can't think of anything to go with eight. The "Aging Eight" keeps coming to mind and that will never go over, will it?

April 26. Haven't we all had this happen to us at one time or another? Margaret went shopping alone and didn't realize until she returned home that she was advertising the name of the store where she'd purchased the new blouse she was wearing. Dangling from her shoulder was the name of the store in bold letters on cardboard attached by one of those unbreakable plastic cords.

I hope this will be a lesson to her. Always, as in swimming, use the buddy system when going shopping.

April 27. Today is my daughter-in-law Mary's birthday. As I've mentioned before, she's a whiz with computers and she also does lovely sewing and needlework. She works part time at the Silver Creek Post Office and part time at the Co-Op store. On top of all this, she's responsible for raising three of my wonderful grandchildren and for loving my favorite son.

April 28. We've been wanting another shade tree in our front yard and decided this was the year of the tree. At our age we'll need to have a very large tree in order to benefit from the shade.

I went tree shopping and found a lovely twelve foot ash tree. It was an adventure for Bob and me to bring Albert (it has to have a name, doesn't it?) home with us in our small pick-up. The wind was blowing 50 miles an hour so we had to tie Albert down with rope. I stuck my arm through the open window and hung onto his upper branches to keep him from jumping ship or jumping pick-up in this case.

As soon as the wind dies down and I can move my arm again we'll let Albert put down permanent roots in his new home.

April 29. There are lots of exotic recipes floating around out there but this one has got to top them all.

It's a South American stew which is to be cooked over an eruption hole at the top of a volcano. Imagine carrying your stew pot filled with the stew ingredients in one hand and a large stirring spoon in the other hand as you climb to the top of the volcano. Just as your stew starts to boil, the volcano erupts and you run like crazy down the side of the volcano beating the hot lava away with your stew stirring spoon.

Yes, I'm sure we'll all give this recipe a try. You go first.

April 30. Unbelievable. It rained a gentle rain throughout the night and now it's snowing beautiful, huge snowflakes. Albert, our new tree, is shivering so excuse me while I go cover him with a blanket.

May 1. May Basket Day. Do you remember when May baskets were so much fun? For days before May First we fashioned all sorts of home-made baskets to put flowers or candy in. The morning of the first day of May was so exciting as May baskets were placed on your friends' and neighbors' front door steps. You knocked on the door and ran to hide behind a bush or tree to see their faces when they answered and spied the May basket. What fun! Do any of the younger people even know what I'm talking about?

May 2. Bob and I've discovered something after many years of marriage. The love has always been there but we were so busy raising our children and earning a living, we didn't realize until Robin and Kevin had left the nest to pursue their own lives, that we have an added bonus in our lives. Bob and I have discovered that we actually like each other.

May 3. Now is as good a time as any to thank Robin for encouraging me to write this book. Thank you daughter.

I also know who I can blame for wasting more than a year of my life if it bombs.

May 4. I find this interesting. We planted Albert, who is twelve-feet tall. Our young neighbors Larry and Brenda have planted a five-foot weeping birch. Pat and Willie who are senior citizens like us, have planted a twelve-foot mountain ash. We all expect to have shade from these trees, so we must have diverse ideas as to what the future has in store for us.

May 5. Bob and I are into the yard thing this year. We went to North Platte and bought a dwarf spruce tree. Now I'd like to have it planted where the forsythia bush is and the forsythia bush moved to another corner of the house. It's really just like moving furniture.

I also have three ornamental leaf plants, eight geraniums, six begonias, and twelve moss rose plants waiting in the house to be moved outside when the weather is warm enough. We're also waiting for eighteen feet of sweet William blankets to arrive in the mail.

That will be all for this year, I promise. Although I did see some lovely gardenia bushes at the greenhouse that caught my eye.

May 6. Willie and Pat gave us a three-foot patch of sod to replace a bad spot in our lawn. Now I'm wondering when it's time to mow that patch, will Willie come over and mow it or is that now our responsibility?

May 7. I went grocery shopping today. An episode occurred which I found amusing, but for which I also had empathy. There was a pleasant lady in front of me at the checkout counter who glanced back at me then looked back again. She said, "Hi, Betty. How are you? I haven't seen you in a long time. How is your mother?"

I said, "I'm fine, but I'm sorry to tell you, my mother passed away two years ago."

She looked at me a little closer and said, "Oh, I'm sorry. I thought you were Betty J. I'm always getting you two mixed up."

I replied, "I know the lady you're thinking of and I'm sorry to inform you that she died a year ago."

Her face took on the look of "Please floor, swallow me whole." As she hurriedly left the store, I caught up with her and said, "Don't feel too bad about the mistaken identity. At least you got my name right."

May 8. I'm wondering how many other senior citizens grew up believing that medicine had to taste bad in order to be good for you. My parents must have bought this stuff by the case. They insisted it cured everything from hangnails to stomach-aches. It was called castor oil, and to this day I'm sure there was never anything else in the world that tasted as bad.

May 9. Today is Doris's birthday. I admire her ability to weather the tragedies she has faced in her life. It amazes me that she's also a rock when someone else has a problem. She has an inner strength that is unequaled by most of us.

May 10. Why do we look forward to the renewal of growing things each spring? We must sadistically enjoy the muscle aches, tired bodies, and blisters we so willingly strive for with planting, weeding, hoeing, watering, mowing, and all else that goes with watching green things grow. Wouldn't it be simpler to paint the whole outdoors into a mural that just needed to be hosed down now and then?

May 11. It's been raining more this May than normal. It was supposed to rain in April but it didn't. They've moved the clocks ahead in the spring and back in the fall so many times that the whole world must be running a month behind by now.

May 12. Mother's Day. To all mothers everywhere have a happy day. I expected the lovely cards and gifts from my kids and grandkids and would've been unpleasantly surprised and ticked off if I'd received nothing. I was pleasantly surprised though, when Kathy my friend and neighbor, knocked on my door today to give me a creeping purple petunia. Try saying that three times fast.

May 13. I gained a pound last Thursday at the birthday coffee Pat had at her home for Doris and that pound is still with me. I don't understand it at all. All I ate was a cinnamon roll, a piece of coffee cake, two pieces of butter brickle bread, and a lemon muffin. It must've been the ham sandwich I ate at supper.

May 14. Today is Primary Election Day in Nebraska. I voted, came home, and pulled weeds. The weeds will come back pretty much the same as they were before. The politicians I voted for will also come back pretty much the same as they were before. Have I just wasted my whole day?

May 15. I must get out in the sun more. My legs look like unbreaded fish sticks.

May 16. Does it ever fail to happen? I mailed a letter to the company that Pat and I had ordered sweet William blankets from, complaining that we hadn't received them. Three hours later, Pat called to tell me they'd just arrived.

Oh well. I guess it'll be all right. In my complaint letter I gave Pat's name and address for the company to refer all their correspondence to.

May 17. Bob and I replaced the mirror I broke in the bathroom. As I was taking the old one down, it broke again. Now does that mean fourteen years of bad luck or does it only count once for only seven years of bad luck? Either way the reflection on this situation is a little grim.

May 18. Nothing unusual happened for me today but each day still brings something to make it special for the young and old alike. It may be seeing a lovely flower, a visit with a friend, a phone call from someone you love, a funny little joke, or a happy memory. Some days don't seem very special, but if we take the time to look outside ourselves, we can enjoy the small pleasures as much as the red letter days.

May 19. I've always heard that flies only live one day. Do millers only live one day, too? I sure hope so because we've been invaded by a horde of alien millers this year and I'm waiting for them to die on their own. I hate to kill them. It has nothing to do with the right to life. I just can't stand that crackly squishy sound you hear and feel when you squash them flat.

May 20. Elaine and I went bargain hunting with Doris today. After taking in a couple of garage sales, we went to the Jumble Shop in Ogallala and I felt like I'd hit the jackpot in Las Vegas. I got a shirt for Bob, two blouses, a pair of slacks, a dress, and a decorative rattan bird cage for only five dollars.

Then we drove about fourteen miles south of Ogallala to the lilac gardens where Max Peterson and his wife have nurtured at least a thousand lilac bushes of many different varieties, colors and scents. It was a walk through a fairyland and probably the best bargain of the day.

May 21. Bob and I were watching a biography of Admiral Byrd on educational television this evening and Bob said, "I've always wanted to explore the world like that but I've always wanted to be home by nightfall."

I guess that explains why he never achieved that goal.

May 22. I just heard on the radio that one of the United States' top ranked basketball stars is asking for a contract renewal of $36,000,000 for the next two years. I don't think anyone is worth that kind of money no matter how great they are.

Isn't this giving the youth of our country the wrong message?

May 23. Last fall when the roofers were shingling our damaged roof, they parked a large truck in our driveway to put the old shingles in. It was blocking the garage door but before they left for the first night, they told me I could move the truck if I needed to get our car out before they returned the next day. As they were leaving the yard, one of them yelled back, "Oh, by the way, the key is broken off in the ignition and the truck has to be started with a wrench."

Since this truck was as tall as the eaves on our house and I would have needed a ladder to even get into the cab, I was leery about starting it. I was afraid if I ever got it started, I'd level Kirk and Sharon's home across the street before I could get the truck stopped. Needless to say, I left the truck and our car exactly where they were until the roofers returned.

May 24. Bob's 50th year high school reunion is this weekend in Big Springs. They have a three day celebration planned beginning with a catered dinner tonight, a social hour, banquet and dance tomorrow night, and a brunch Sunday morning. These people are no longer as young as they once were. It will be interesting to see how many will still be as active three days from now as they are today.

May 25. What a full day this has been. The Memorial Day weekend is a big event in Big Springs. The day begins at 7:30 in the morning with a 5K and one-mile run throughout the town.

At 8:00, the Memorial Hall opens with booths for crafts, cotton candy, funnel cakes, Mexican food, baked goods, T-shirt and cap sales, cosmetics, raffles, personalized children's books, and an outdoor barbecue.

At 1:30 in the afternoon, there is country gospel singing and at 2:00 golf cart races are held. During these activities, the Phelps Hotel has a quilt showing and tour and the Big Springs Museum is open for viewing.

At 6:30 the alumni banquet is held at the high school followed by a public dance at the Memorial Hall to finish off the day.

Bob's 50th year class alumni were honored guests at the banquet. In a crowd of 280, his class was well represented with twenty-two classmates and their spouses attending. Pretty good for a graduating class of twenty-eight. As I was dressing to go to this event, my earring fell apart so I glued it together and hastily put it on. My necklace and earrings were strands of thousands of tiny, black crystal beads. Halfway through the banquet my necklace broke. I was wearing a scooped neck dress and hundreds of tiny black crystal beads trickled into my neckline to lodge next to my skin all over my body. I removed what was left of my necklace from around my neck and with only slight fidgeting finished the evening.

I learned two lessons from this evening. When you have beads stuck all over your skin, undressing should be done while standing in a wastebasket. Picking hundreds of tiny black crystal beads out of a carpet is very time consuming.

The second lesson is this: When you wear an earring that has been glued, be sure the glue is dry before attaching it to your ear. I had glued my earring to my ear and when I removed the earring, part of my ear came off with it.

May 26. Guess what new law the powers-that-be want to enforce now. They want to make it mandatory for rodeo bull-riders to wear helmets. I just can't see this going over unless they shape the helmets like Western hats.

May 27. Today is Memorial Day. A time to remember loved ones no longer with us. I miss all our family and friends who have gone before us but the one I miss most is a little boy I never knew. He is my grandson Jason who didn't have his chance at life on earth. I know he's one of the sweetest little angels in heaven.

May 28. Some days are like this. I had an appointment to have my hair done at 8:00 A.M. Wrong. When I got to Tiny's she said, "Hi Betty. What are you doing here now? Your appointment isn't until 1:00 this afternoon."

Well, that was only the beginning. I thought I'd scheduled my day quite well. Wrong.

I backed my day up a little, went home, fixed my hair, and proceeded to go to Julesburg to do some necessary shopping. I'd made the checks out accordingly before I left home to save time at the stores. Wrong. I gave Tiny's check to the druggist, the druggist's check to the grocery store, and the grocery store check to the variety store. So, back to square one. Halfway home I remembered I was supposed to go to the hardware store. More backtracking.

I wonder if all this has anything to do with that mirror I broke. How long will I be able to blame all my goof-ups on that mirror?

May 29. For years I had Bob believing it was impossible to replace a zipper in a sweatshirt once it had broken. That was until Pat mentioned within Bob's hearing range that she'd just replaced a zipper in a jacket.

I knew it would come. The day Bob asked me if Pat could replace the zippers in two of his sweatshirts, I said enthusiastically, "Oh, we won't bother Pat. I can do it."

First I bought the zippers, one black and one tan, and discovered the ones he wanted replaced were both tan. I fixed one sweatshirt with a zipper that was too short, broke one sewing machine needle, and ran another needle through my finger. I then made another trip to town to buy a longer zipper to repair sweatshirt number two. Arriving back home, I found that this zipper was two inches too long.

I was right in the first place. It is impossible to replace a zipper in a sweatshirt — for me anyway.

May 30. I find this hard to believe but the *Farmer's Almanac* admits that it doesn't know everything. It doesn't know for example, why there are interstate highways in Hawaii.

May 31. Did you know that a grapefruit usually has an average of thirteen sections? Once in a great while, there are only twelve and on rare days fourteen. Today was a red letter day. As I cut Bob's grapefruit for his breakfast for the first time that I can remember his grapefruit had fifteen sections.

I know. I need to get a life.

June

June 1. I had nightmares all night long. I seriously doubt if the chocolate stars, tomato, and banana I ate just before retiring had anything to do with it. But have you ever been chased by a creature with a banana body, a tomato head, and chocolate star eyes?

June 2. I wonder why people can't get along better with each other. Birds can't fly with only one feather. It takes different kinds of feathers working together and each feather has a role in giving a bird the thrill of flight. If all people worked together like a bird's feathers, I'm confident we could accomplish wondrous things in this world.

June 3. Did you know they found a page from a speech George Washington wrote under a sofa in a home in England? That speech was written 200 years ago. I thought I was careless with my house cleaning habits but I feel a lot better about them now.

June 4. As you grow older, you sometimes do dumb things, like putting the garbage in the refrigerator. One nice thing about growing older is that you soon forget what it was that you did that was so dumb in the first place. I can't remember where I put the bag of garbage that I had this morning and I've already checked the cupboards. I guess I'll just have to get brave and open the refrigerator door to see if that's where I stored it this time.

June 5. Do men realize what a difficult job shopping is for women? First you must choose your wardrobe carefully. Your clothing and shoes need to allow your movements to be swift. This is especially true in garage sale shopping. Driving around a block for hours is also time consuming—but it must be done—until you find a parking space within a few yards of the stores and sales you need to get to.

Once inside the stores, the decisions are endless. It's taxing to your brain cells and often produces shopping headaches. Once the decisions are made, you are lucky if you can get into the longest checkout line. You strive for this much needed rest for your mind and body.

Having gathered all your purchases, it's time to head for home where all the carrying in, sorting out, and putting away begins. By then you're completely exhausted. Men really think women enjoy going through all this.

June 6. I have decided the letters OLD do not mean aged. Depending on your gender they either mean "one lovable doll" or "one lovable dude."

June 7. My Uncle Walt stopped by and gave me a beautiful porcelain bell with a fragile porcelain hummingbird and flower perched on top. It touched my heart. It also made me wonder about omens, because only a few minutes before he came I'd been watching a hummingbird drink nectar from the flowers growing on our front porch.

June 8. The following is an unbiased critique of this book and one I plan to have framed and hung on the wall.

"This is so great. I love it. I feel like I'm listening to Maxine, Ann Landers, Erma Bombeck and Archie Bunker's wife Edith, all rolled into one. It makes me laugh. It makes me cry. It sounds like a great movie. Love, Your daughter, Robin."

June 9. Life is like a chain letter. What you give of yourself returns to you tenfold. I hope this year-long chain letter has made my family and friends smile. I hope that those who don't know me personally will feel a kinship.

Writing this journal has been one of the most rewarding times of my life. I've learned these are not the sunset years of my life after all — for everyday brings a bright new sunshine. Growing older is a blessed gift. It gives us all the reflections of yesterday and all the wonders of tomorrow.

To Order More Copies of
And How Was Your Day?...

Please send:

_____copies of _____
(Title of book)

at $ _____each TOTAL _____

Nebr. residents add 6.5% sales tax_____

Shipping/Handling
$3.00 for first book.
$1.00 for each additional book. _____

TOTAL ENCLOSED   _____

Name _____

Address _____

City _____State _____Zip _____

☐ Visa ☐ Master Card
Credit card number _____

Expiration date _____

Order by credit card, personal check or money order.
Send to:

Dageforde Publishing, Inc.
Mail Order Dept.
941 'O' Street, Suite 706
Lincoln, NE 68508
Or, order **TOLL FREE: 800-216-8794**